THINKING WITH HORSES

THINKING WITH HORSES

by

HENRY BLAKE

Trafalgar Square Publishing

NORTH POMFRET, VERMONT

First published 1977 by Souvenir Press Ltd,
43 Great Russell Street, London WC1B 3PA
and simultaneously in Canada by
Methuen Publications,
Agincourt, Ontario
Reprinted 1993, 1994

First published in paperback in the United States of America
in 1993 by Trafalgar Square Publishing, North Pomfret,
Vermont 05053.

ISBN 0-943955-79-3

Library of Congress Catalog Card Number: 93-60185

Printed in Great Britain by
The Guernsey Press Co. Ltd, Guernsey, Channel Islands

Contents

1: *Early Guesses About Horse Psychology*

As a Rugby player I had more enthusiasm than skill. But never-theless, I managed to get my first fifteen cap, and on 20th October 1945 I played for my school against Wells. By a piece of good fortune the ball was kicked ahead and I tore up the field to find myself on the twenty-five-yard line with the ball at my feet and no one between me and the line. So I trapped the ball with my knees, controlled it, and dribbled like hell. Unfortunately the opposing fullback who had been left standing came tearing up behind me and tried to fall on the ball. But he fell on my leg instead, and smashed my knee to smithereens. I spent the next three months on my back in plaster, and then nine months on crutches. This at the age of sixteen, was a shattering blow. And for a healthy young animal, who was fit and used to running about, being confined to bed was the worst punishment imagin-able. But it gave me a very, very great advantage over my fellows, because for the first time in my life I had nothing to do but think or read. And since you can only read so many books a day, I had to do quite a lot of thinking. An unusual pastime at sixteen.

I had a very nice three-year-old mare that I was working just before my accident. But unfortunately she had two very bad curbs on her hocks, so the decision was made that she had to be fired. This was done at the end of February, just after I was beginning to hobble around on crutches. Nothing could steady the mare enough to allow her to have the operation done. Time and time again the vet and the assistants came out of the stable door in a bundle, and eventually I could stand it no longer. I pegged in on my crutches and talked to her for a couple of minutes, and then went and leant against her hindquarters. The vet, who was a man of quick decision and action, walked straight

7

in, carried out the operation, and the mare didn't move. I made a great fuss of her, collected my crutches and went out into the sunlight feeling very pleased with myself.

Unfortunately a couple of days later, trying to do more than I should have done on my crutches, I went head over heels, smashed my plaster and was banished to my bed again. Lying on my back gazing at the same blue wall, the same cracks in the ceiling, and the same hole in my counterpane I had studied for the previous three months, I began to wonder why the mare had behaved quietly when I was leaning against her, and not before. I had always known that I had what might be termed the 'green finger' with horses: unrideable horses would go calmly and easily for me, when they deposited my brothers and sister unceremoniously on the ground. I had accepted this as just one of those things. But the firing operation on the filly made me think. Why had she been so compliant for me? It can't have been maternal instinct that made her protect me: three-year-old fillies don't have much maternal instinct, since they have never been mothers. And I was honest enough with myself to know that I hadn't given her all that much cause to love me. I had ridden her hard, and made her jump when she didn't want to jump. Admittedly I had made a fuss of her when she had done the right thing, and I fed and looked after her. But as an unpleasant, bad mannered, bad tempered sixteen-year-old, I hadn't given anybody or anything much cause to love me. So why had it been more important to the filly to accept a certain discomfort herself from the operation, rather than risk hurting my injured leg? How had she even known that I was injured? I decided that she had sensed my injury. But the only possible reason for her to protect me, was that I belonged to her. That I was hers. I had already noticed that when I was with a group of other horses she would try to keep herself between me and the other animals. And it came as rather a shock to a young man who had looked upon himself as the Lord of Creation that he actually belonged to an unsound three-year-old filly.

When I was allowed out of bed and started hobbling around on my crutches again, I began watching the other horses as well.

To try and see what made them tick. I noticed that when the horses were being turned out of the yard, always the same horses led the way, and the others kept more or less at the back. It wasn't the fastest horse in the front, and it wasn't the first one out of the stable that went away in front. It was always old Fearless who led the others out of the yard. And it was always Champion who shepherded them along from behind.

What made Caravan, who was three times as fast as Fearless, and a much faster walker, walk slowly behind her? And when the horses were in the field I noticed that if something alarmed them, it was usually Chester who would go and investigate. Why if an object was frightening enough to scare Firefly into trotting away, did Chester trot over to see what the trouble was?

All these problems, and hundreds of others, started to interest me. And one of the advantages of studying horses is that they are such sympathetic animals, that they very quickly let you know whether you are right or wrong. They let you know the food they like or don't like, by either eating it greedily, or spitting it out. They let you know how much food they want by the way they eat it, or by the way their condition responds. If you do something they like, they'll show their pleasure. If you do something they don't like, they'll kick your flaming teeth in. If you ride them in the right way, they'll go beautifully for you. But if you do the wrong things, they'll tell you by going badly for you.

These reflections set me thinking a great deal about what lay behind the behaviour of horses, and I learned to verify my guesses by devising tests of their reactions.

For example, I decided that Caravan was so excitable and unpredictable in harness because nobody trusted him. And so methodically for the next week I made a great show of trusting Caravan implicitly – at the same time making damned sure that I was near enough to grab his head if he looked like going off with the cart. And Caravan acted like an angel. So one gloriously sunny June day I was sent down to the river with Caravan, plus four forty-gallon drums, to haul water for the cattle. We went out of the gate and stopped to chat to the stonemason who was busy facing the stone gate post which Caravan had demolished in one of his previous escapades. And he said, 'Don't knock this down again.' And I said, 'Oh no! I've got this horse right now, he is going absolutely beautifully. He won't do it again.' So very carefully and sedately Caravan and I jogged gently down the road with the four forty-gallon drums clanking and banging in the float. We got down to the bottom, and it was absolutely glorious, the river was beautiful, the willows were breathtaking with their delicate green and the sound of the water was extremely enticing. So I decided that when I had filled the drums, I'd have a quick swim. Dreaming of this I got out of the float and went to open the gate into the long meadow. And as I got the gate open I heard a rattle, and I was just quick enough to see Caravan turn the float in the road and go hell for leather back the half-mile to the farm yard. I followed in fear and trembling. And as I came around the corner, there in front of me was the new gate post, scattered over an area of about twenty yards. Caravan had proved to me that I was wrong. He wasn't untrustworthy because he wasn't trusted, but just because he got bored pulling a cart.

At that time we had a particularly savage bull, and moving him and the heifers from one field to another was extremely difficult and dangerous, since he would charge very nearly any-one, mounted or on foot. But I said I thought Caravan would enjoy the excitement of doing it, and I'd do the job myself. This wasn't bravery or stupidity as everyone thought. The fact was that I had the choice of doing that, (and I thought if I was crafty I could take most of the day over it) or picking early potatoes. And anyway I decided that if the bull did have a go at us, Caravan was quick enough on his feet to get me out of trouble.

My father was reluctant to agree. But it was either that or having everyone stop picking potatoes for half a day to move the stock, and anyway I had been courting death for sixteen years and survived it, so Caravan and I set off to our task. With the potato digger clanking away behind us, it wasn't a job to be hurried. I rode down to the field, and sat on Caravan studying the problem for half an hour. The cattle had to be moved out of the field into a lane, down the lane a quarter of a mile and then into one of the river fields. The main problems were first to get the bull out of the field, second to stop the cattle taking the wrong turning at the end of the lane, and third to make sure they didn't go past the open gateway into the river field. After half an hour or so the answer came to me. We had always driven them out before, and although the heifers always moved towards the gateway, sometimes slowly, sometimes going hell for leather, when we came to move the bull, he charged whoever went towards him. The answer to the problem suddenly became obvious: to make the bull charge. So I opened the two gates into the field and rode towards the bull. When he saw me coming, he put his head down and started roaring, bellowing, and pawing the ground. I rode towards him at a slight angle, shouting at him, he bellowed louder and started coming towards me with his head down. So I turned Caravan away slightly, still shouting at the bull, and eventually his rage got too much for him and he charged. I put my heels to Caravan and went flat out for the gate. The bull hurled himself after us for the best part of a hundred yards, and slowed down. So I went back and did the same thing again. This time the bull's charge carried him right out into the lane. I cantered a further hundred yards down the lane, popped Caravan over the fence into the next field, and left the bull to its own devices. With no one to annoy him he set to work raking the bank with his horns, but I didn't mind about that. I'd got him out of the field.

Caravan thought this was wonderful fun. He was dancing and cavorting all over the place. We popped over the fence back into the field where the heifers were, making quick work of rounding them up and driving them out after the bull. Some had already followed, but the rest of them went out in a bunch at a rush, and the poor bull didn't know what was happening as they charged by him. As soon as I had seen the last of the heifers out of the field, I jumped the two or three hedges parallel to the lane, and dropped off the bank down into the road just in front of the heifers so that they shot down the lane, with the bull going willy nilly in the middle of the mob. As soon as they were all in the road, again I set Caravan alight and we went flat-out down the verge to pass the bunch before they shot past the field. I pulled up just past the gate in a clatter of sliding hoofs, and swung Caravan round just in time to turn the leading heifers into the field. The whole mob wheeled in like a squad of soldiers. Caravan stood watching them with his head and tail raised, and nostrils cracking. His pleasure in a job well done was clear to see. In actual fact we had taken less than a quarter of an hour on a task that would normally have taken seven or eight people half a day. I shut the gate, and rode Caravan the couple of hundred yards on to my favourite bathing pool, where I took his saddle and bridle off and turned him loose to graze and roll, while I spent the next two-and-a-half hours alternately bathing in the cold stinging river water, and lying in the sun in my birthday suit letting the sun warm me. The stolen pleasure was enhanced by the occasional sounds of the digger, reminding us that everyone else, men and horses, were doing a hard dirty task.

This story is told as an illustration of the fact that if your guess about what motivates animal behaviour is right, the rewards can be very great. If your guess is wrong of course, you have to pay the penalty, but the more you study what makes a horse tick, the better you get to know it, the more likely you are to be right.

This escapade with Caravan started me thinking again. If the understanding of a horse's motives could help me escape a morning's potato digging, I might be able to turn it to financial advantage as well. One of my principal sources of income during the summer months was from gymkhanas. I had quite a useful gymkhana pony that I took to two or three gymkhanas a week, and which made me a reasonable income already. But if I could understand what made Chester a good gymkhana pony, and what

made her win, could I not make her win more often, and so increase our winnings? Could I not increase her *will* to win?

Now I knew one of the reasons why Chester was a good
gymkhana pony was that *I* worked extremely hard at it, and
put in an awful lot of schooling. And I thought there lazing on
the river bank that it was quite possible that I had been over-
schooling her: that I had been working her so hard that the
work was becoming monotonous, and her enthusiasm was dwind-
ling. So to see if my theory was right, I didn't work her for the
next couple of days. When I took her to the gymkhana on the
Saturday she was jumping out of her skin. She went extremely
well and won more than her usual share of the prize money.

I also worked out that one of her motives for winning was
that she wanted to please me, so that if I could make her want
to please me more, she would want to win more. And so over
the next three weeks I made a great point of making a great
fuss of her when she won, and ignoring her when she didn't.
It certainly seemed to improve her performance, though it was
difficult to be absolutely certain how much of the improved performance was due to the fact that she wanted to please me and
how much to the fact that she wasn't being worked quite so
hard, and so was enjoying her work more. But the proof that
working on her affection for me had paid off came about three
weeks later, at Chinnock Gymkhana in the Gretna Green race.

The Gretna Green race at this time was quite simple: one
person stood at the end of the field, while his partner, in this
case a girlfriend of mine who always worked with me in this
event, led the two horses down. Then the person on foot got
on his own horse and they had to ride back hand in hand. On
this occasion Biddy, to get a quick start, stationed herself and the
two horses next to the starter. Unfortunately the starter was
too enthusiastic, and he accidentally brought his flag down very
hard across Chester's nose. Chester reared up, hung back, and
smashed her bridle, and there was Biddy with her horse, and
my bridle, but no horse on the other end of it. I saw what happened, and bellowed at the top of my voice: 'Chester.' She

pricked her ears, saw me, and galloped straight down the field, with Biddy in hot pursuit. When Chester got to me she skidded to a halt. I pushed her round so that she was pointing in the right direction, jumped on her back just as Biddy came up with bridle, and her own pony, and away we went back to the finishing line, winning quite easily because Biddy had had no horse to lead.

There was some muttering afterwards about the way we had won, but it was quite legal: Biddy and both horses had come down to meet me, and the fact that on the way back my bridle was draped around Biddy on her pony and not on my pony's head was a very minor technicality. Chester's affection for me had indeed paid dividends. In fact over the last five weeks of the holidays, my income went up by nearly thirty percent, which proved to me without a shadow of doubt that the effort of trying to understand a horse's motives was extremely profitable.

Over the next two or three years I tried to increase this understanding. And other questions began to come to my mind. Exactly what for instance were the horse's physical needs? What other needs did they have? How did horses see things, and what did horses feel? And above all, what was it that made horses *different*? Horses, I was noticing increasingly, might come from the same place, with very similar parentage, and behave in completely different ways. On occasions even full brothers would react in opposite ways to a sudden noise; or a pat on the neck.

Whether I would ever have gone on to more serious research into horse psychology were it not for the death of a man called Hughes, I am not sure. But Mr Hughes died at the ripe old age of seventy-nine, and among the effects he left behind were three unbroken colts that he had bred out of the same mare by a stallion called Pollards.

I was a young man, newly married and set up on my own, when a friend of mine called John Jeffries bought these three colts from the widow, and asked me to break them. This I did, somewhat haphazardly, but I got them going nice and quietly, and he offered, instead of paying me for my work in cash, to give me an unbroken thirteen-two pony. I was agreeable, broke the pony, and took it to Exeter Market. Having sold her quite well, I stood around watching the other horses being sold with the money for the pony burning a hole in my pocket. A very nice fourteen-three skewbald gelding came into the ring which no one seemed to have a great interest in, so I bought him quite cheaply and left myself with the magnificent sum of thirty bob change. I took him back to his pen and was just putting him in, when someone came up and offered me a profit of ten pounds, which I very quickly took, and he took him home. (What I didn't know, and he didn't know of course, was that the pony was a rig. He had had him home about three days when the local riding school went past. The pony took one look at the classy filly that the owner of the riding school was riding, realised that the mare was in season, jumped the fence and chased the whole riding school right through the middle of Torquay, eventually obtaining the object of his desire in the main street. But that's another story.)

I, with seventy-one pound notes in my pocket, plus the thirty bob change I had from my previous transaction, was really on the ball looking for a horse to make a fortune out of. I went looking for Tim Horgan, who was a very old friend of mine and had been selling horses to my father for the previous thirty years. He always had a string of Irish horses at every sale, and when I got there he was busy selling a very nice four-year-old to an enthusiastic farmer. 'Sure he's a grand horse! Look at the size of him! And he's so quiet you could put your mother on him!' This went on for about ten minutes with Tim expanding on the virtues of the horse and its quietness and gentleness, until the sale was completed. The new owner went off to get a bridle and saddle.

'Is he quiet, Tim?' 'Sure enough.' 'Yes,' I said, 'but how quiet is he when you ride him?' 'Oh, we will know won't we when me laddo gets on his back,' Tim replied. When the young man returned, I assisted Tim and the new owner to saddle the horse, which may or may not have had a saddle on his back before, but he didn't appear to worry, and when the boy got on his back and rode him out of the yard he went quite quietly, though it was obvious that he didn't really know what bit and bridle were for.

After we had seen him disappear from view quite safely I told Tim what I was looking for. Most of the horses he had were too expensive for me. But he had one which looked just what I wanted. She was a well bred mare, about fifteen-three. But Tim was very cagey about her. 'Has she been ridden Tim?' 'Sure she's had a saddle on her.' 'How quiet is she?' 'That I wouldn't know.' 'But she is a six-year-old mare, Tim! She must have done a bit of work!' 'Sure she has done a bit of work!' Even in his desire to sell the horse, Tim was still being extremely cagey but eventually I bought her for sixty quid, and having had a very profitable day I took my new purchase home.

We were very fortunate that the mare was by a stallion which had been standing near my wife's home, so we 'phoned a friend of hers to make enquiries. An hour later he telephoned back. 'For God's sake, get rid of the bloody animal. She has been in every yard in Cork, and no one could ride her.' Every word Tim had said was true: she had done a lot of work. She had been long-reined, she had been lunged – in fact she had been lunged for four hours on end at times – she had had a saddle on her back. She had even had someone sitting on the saddle for up to two minutes. But she was unrideable.

This was just the sort of stimulus that I needed. The mare was a challenge. The following day we made a start on her. And this didn't mean taking her out on a lunging rein, and belting around until she was too tired to stand. Nor did it mean starving her, or keeping her short of water. Making a start on a horse like this in our book meant getting to know the horse, and getting the horse to know and trust you.

We called her Starry because she had a white star on her forehead. For the first day or two working with Starry meant standing in the stable dodging her heels. But eventually we established some sort of truce, enough for her to allow me to go into the stable, or walk up to her and make a fuss of her. And then I got Leslie, my very pregnant wife, to give me a leg up, and I stayed there for a minute or two. Starry of course didn't have a bridle or a saddle on, just a rope head collar, and she didn't object too much. So I slipped off. On again, off. On again. The third time I eased myself up, instead of just leaning across her. I eased my leg over and sat up. And she stood quite quietly, still eating out of the bucket in the manger. So I told my wife to take the bucket out and use it to lead her out of the stable door. This she did and proceeded up the lane until Starry had finished the nuts in the bucket, at which point I very quickly stopped the mare, slid off and led her home again.

We did this for three days, riding her without a bridle or a saddle and just letting her follow the bucket with her breakfast up the road. I decided then that the mare had become quite civilized, so I put a saddle and a bridle on and got on to her. Or to be more exact I started to get on to her: I got my foot in the stirrup and was half way across the saddle before I landed in the dung heap. Since my wife's pregnancy didn't allow for much athletics and there was obviously going to be a great deal of athletics, I telephoned my father to come and give me a hand.

Since he and my stepmother were entertaining some very stuffy relatives for tea, he didn't need a second invitation, and about an hour later we made another start with Starry. This time my father held her head whilst I got on, and holding her very tight by the bridle, led her up the road to the nearest field. As soon as we got inside the gateway, he pointed her up the hill and leant against the gate post to enjoy the rodeo. And a rodeo he had. I could see then why the mare had been in every yard in Cork: she had learnt a new trick for getting people off in every one of them. She bucked in a straight line, she bucked up and down on one spot, she bucked around in a tight circle. She tried to get my legs by galloping up the fencing posts. But eventually, after a large number of falls, she and I came to a working arrangement: she wouldn't buck me off if I didn't kick her in the ribs. And since it was nearly my milking time we left it at that.

My father came over the following morning to work her again, and we had another rodeo. But it was only a third as vigorous as the first day, and on the third day, apart from two or three episodes of bucking and one of going flat-out with me straight into a hedge, she went extremely well. After about ten days I could ride her out of the yard with reasonable confidence that I'd still be in the saddle when I came back.

But there was no pleasure in riding her. She was extremely sullen, bad tempered and lethargic. If she couldn't buck and get me off she just sulked.

On the tenth day the horse that I was playing polo on went lame, which meant that I was short of something to ride that afternoon. So we took Starry instead. When we got to the polo ground I got on her, and had a very short rodeo before riding her out to play in a slow chukka of polo. For the first couple of minutes she was her sulky, miserable self. And then she suddenly began to realize what was happening, and for the first time since we had had her she cantered and galloped without bucking. I rode her in a second chukka at the end of the afternoon, and she began to go happily and willingly. At the end of a fortnight the transformation in Starry was complete. From a miserable, sullen, sulky bitch she had become a sweet, kind and happy pony. And she just loved polo.

I asked myself why a horse which people had been trying unsuccessfully to break for three years, and which I had found impossible to get working with any degree of amiability, should change in a fortnight and eight or ten chukkas of polo into a model of all that was sweet, kind and willing? The key of course was that she enjoyed playing polo – which was not extraordinary since most polo ponies love the game. So it wasn't very difficult to reason out that she had been refusing to be ridden because her experience of being ridden had not been enjoyable, so she couldn't see any pleasure in it. But once she understood that being ridden meant that she could enjoy herself doing something that she liked doing, she was quite happy for anyone to sit on her back.

This is what started me thinking about what we knew about a horse's body, and what we could deduce about its needs and desires. We knew for example that its hearing is much the same as ours, whilst the shape of its eye means that it sees objects differently. This latter is of less consequence than it seems, since if you always saw a tree looking like a sausage, when you saw an object looking like a sausage you would know it was a tree: trees in short would always have the same appearance. So though a horse's eyesight is different from ours, we have no reason to assume that its ability to distinguish objects or categories of objects by sight is very different. We knew also that the horse's tolerance to heat and cold are much the same as man's, but that its feeding habits are different, the horse being vegetarian and man omnivorous.

As for the sexual needs of horses, we knew that the needs of the mare are less than those of the woman, since the mare comes into season only for a short period each month and hardly at all during the winter months. The heat period is only three or four days a month, compared with the twenty-four to twenty-five days a month for a woman. But the intensity of the heat when it comes is for that very reason bound to be greater, and the stress caused by that heat far more intense. As for males, we were mainly in contact with geldings, but they still have a certain amount of sexual drive, although this varies considerably from gelding to gelding.

These, as we saw them, were the horse's bodily needs. But we knew that horses had other needs as well, and that if we were to understand more of what made our horses tick, we had to discover what these needs were.

We had an example of one of them almost immediately. My hunter Honesty nearly severed her near fore tendon on a sheet of galvanized zinc, which meant that we had to have her in.

But she had a special friend, my point-to-pointer, Weeping Roger, and he at that time was out to grass, relaxing after a strenuous season of racing. We couldn't have him in as well, so we turned a pony out with him, which meant that he was reasonably happy and contented, but Honesty, in one of the loose boxes, immediately began to lose condition. She wasn't eating and her coat became dull. At first we put this down to the injury she had received, but her leg healed quickly, and still Honesty wasn't eating. We tried tempting her with bits of green from the garden – I went out cutting grass for her. But she showed her disdain for it by dunging on top of it. Still she lost condition, and still she refused to eat. We didn't find the key to the problem until one day we had to catch my daughter's pony to have it shod. Since he was a little devil to catch, we caught him the day before the blacksmith came and pushed him in Honesty's loose box for the night. I went out about ten o'clock to make sure that he wasn't bullying Honesty, and saw to my surprise that not only had she eaten her feed, but all her hay. So I put some more in, and went to bed. The following morning Honesty had eaten up all her previous night's feed, and she ate her breakfast like a starving man eating his last meal.

We shod Paddy's pony (he was extremely difficult to shoe, and since he was very small we put him down, rolled him over on his back and I sat on his chest whilst the blacksmith hammered the nails on to the legs sticking up in the air), and I turned him out again.

I put Honesty's feed in again, feeling pleased that at last she had started eating. But she didn't touch it. At last the penny dropped. So we spent the whole afternoon catching Paddy's pony again, and as soon as we put him in with her, she ate.

What had been causing the trouble, of course, was the fact that Honesty was an extremely sociable horse, and when she was deprived of companionship she had no desire to eat. She was getting into a state of depression. She didn't want to do anything. And this experience gave me a new insight into the range of drives and emotions and motives and needs that make up horse personality. This complex of feelings makes a horse what he is. And finding out exactly what these feelings were and how they inter-related was going to be long and difficult. But I realized that if I *could* understand and interpret them, I could make use of them to get better results for myself and to make my horses happy.

Another point that began to become increasingly clear was that there were a number of things that a horse wanted, and needed, which were on the face of it completely unnatural to him. For example, we knew that our horses loved jumping, that they wanted, and needed to jump. Now this is completely unnatural to the horse in the wild, so we decided that there must be a whole series of drives within the horse which arise not from nature but from conditioning, from the training *we* gave. Racing, playing polo, jumping and hunting were all examples. It was our training that made a horse want to beat other horses racing, to enjoy the scrimmage and rough and tumble of playing polo, to put in the extra little bit of effort that is needed in a good jumper. Some of our horses got so excited that they would refuse to eat on hunting mornings. None of these things was to be found in wild horses.

Then, just as we were digesting this lesson, came a time when we had a series of minor accidents among the horses. Accidents and injuries in horses come in phases. One may go for weeks, months or even years, and have no trouble at all, and then suddenly you no sooner heal one wound than you have another one, you no sooner have one lame horse sound than another is hobbling around on three legs.

This time one of the ponies banged his eye. Since there was a real risk that he would go blind, part of his treatment was to keep him in a darkened loose box. This we did for ten days or a fortnight, and after about the third day, I noticed he was becoming extremely bad tempered. After a week he was going mad every time you opened the door, trying to rush out. By the time his injured eye was healed, he seemed to be almost round the bend. But as soon as we began turning him out for an hour at dusk, he started settling down again. And gradually as the days went by, he was allowed out more and more in daylight, and after a week he was completely normal.

I attributed this behaviour at the time to the fact that he had been deprived of light, and subsequent work has verified my opinion. I also noticed that when a horse was tied up he never stood still, but changed from one leg to another, stepping forward a step, stepping backwards a step. So, as well as the need for light, he had a need for movement. And so we had to discover what might be termed the needs for mental stimulus: light, movement, a changing scene. These we saw as among the horse's inherited needs.

We eventually categorized the needs of the horse in four groups. The first comprised the bodily needs, such as food and water, warmth and sex. Next came other 'natural' needs, for movement, for light, and external stimulus. Third were what might be termed the social needs of the horse, for the company and understanding of his companions. And finally there was the fourth group, the conditioned needs that had come about from training by man.

But how could we recognize them, since we couldn't see them? And how, if we were meeting the needs right, were we to know?

We could continue with the method of trial and error, trying this and trying that. But this was very time-consuming, and at times even painful.

One spring, for example, I had a rather sour, bad-tempered horse which I was racing. After considerable thought I came to the conclusion he might be sullen because he didn't like men, and he might therefore go much better for a woman. So my ever-loving, and pregnant wife said she would try him in a gallop and see. One morning with great difficulty we hoisted her five-foot-one, and her pregnant tum, up on to the big sixteen-two horse. Once she was there, with the large spread around the middle, she was reasonably stable, so we rode the two miles up to the gallop, with Wolsey walking along apparently quite happily.

We got to the gallop and lined up, and I said 'go.' Away we went. Slowly increasing our pace on the slow gallop to three-parts speed, Wolsey settled down and lengthened his stride. But after we had gone about half a mile he decided a pregnant tum bouncing up and down on the back of his neck wasn't comfortable, so he proceeded to put in a colossal series of bucks. Leslie settled back quite happily, enjoying the transition from the pounding gallop to a rocking-horse motion, but unfortunately her stirrup leather broke in the midst of a powerful buck, and she started to slide off to one side. All should have been well: she would have slipped off, and that would have been that. But unfortunately her tummy stuck on the saddle, and she was half of her on one side, half on the other, and she couldn't go either way. I galloped alongside, shouting helpful instructions such as 'Get back on,' 'Stop him,' 'Slide off.' All of which was to no avail, and I was told so in no uncertain terms. But eventually, chance took a hand, as Wolsey stumbled over a large anthill and Leslie described a neat parabola straight into a gorse bush. And since the language that came out of the gorse bush was descriptive and very blasphemous, I took myself and my horse off to catch Wolsey, who was grazing about two hundred yards away. Wolsey had shown his opinion of lady riders in no uncertain terms. When we got back to the gorse bush, I put Leslie on to my horse, and rode the miscreant home, whilst Leslie told me what she thought of me, my race horses, and that gorse bush.

Thus it became imperative that we should improve our communication with our horses by some method other than guesses tested by trial and error.

2: *We Learn To Communicate With Horses*

We were making a rather slow beginning with our work on communication with horses,* when, after the birth of our first daughter, I bought a horse for my wife. He was a fifteen-two brown gelding, and when I bought him for twenty-six guineas at Exeter Market, he was more or less unmanageable. We called him Cork Beg, and from the very beginning we both found that we had a special affinity with him. We could understand his feelings, convey our feelings to him as it were instinctively, and anticipate his actions and reactions.

And he started us observing and trying to understand how he conveyed and received messages to and from other horses. At this stage we weren't making much headway, because we made the same mistake as everyone else looking at animal communication: we were trying to put a set meaning to each sound used by a horse.

There are a few sounds that can be made sense of in this way: for example, a mare calling her foal to her, or reassuring the foal, uses a very distinctive sound. But by and large we found that there was very little consistency between one horse's use of a sound, and another's. Shortly after we acquired Cork Beg, however, we made what I considered to be our major breakthrough in animal communication.

One night I was unable to sleep, and during the long watches I started thinking about this and that, as people do. One of the things I was turning over in my mind was whether the apparent stupidity of the *au pair* girl who was helping my wife out with the baby was really natural stupidity, bloody-mindedness, or

* For an account of this see my earlier book *Talking with Horses*, Souvenir Press, 1976.

24

simply inability to understand plain English. The girl had come from Italy and although she could read and write English fluently, she seemed to find it very difficult to understand us. It occurred to me that the problem really arose in interpreting the nods, the grunts and the murmurs which constitute conversation between most human beings, and which vary according to language and culture and even among families and individuals. Language, in short, was not a question of sounds only – it was a whole complex of verbal and non-verbal communication, some of it highly individual and dependent on familiarity for its comprehension. It was exactly the same problem we were facing with the horse.

So it was that I realized that each horse has his own individual language, just as each human being does. He uses sounds to convey various meanings, and anyone who knows him will be able to understand, but there is no set pattern of sound, just as there is no common pattern of sound in the vast variety of human languages.

Even among four people speaking the same language – such as English – you might find four different ways of expressing agreement, for example. One might agree with you by saying 'aye'; one might say 'yes'; one nod his head; and one just grunt 'mm, mm.' You would know they meant that they all agreed with you. But they would be using three different sounds, and one sign, to mean exactly the same thing. So it is with our horses. So we began to make a list of the messages we understood, such as 'Where's my bloody breakfast?', which is the phrase we use when a horse wants food, and to set out the various ways in which each horse conveyed that message: Cork Beg says this by a wicker, Weeping Roger says it by banging his bowl; Starlight says it by shaking her head up and down, and so on. We very quickly had a list of ways that a horse might use to communicate a single message, and we found that the variations around a particular meaning were not very great. We found by this means we could begin to make a pattern of horse vocabulary.

Over the next ten to fifteen years we discovered that the horse uses eleven distinctive notes to convey a message by sound.

These vary from a low snuffle to a scream of rage, fear or pain. But we also discovered that it was pointless to consider sound only in trying to understand horse communication for a horse uses signals and body movements just as frequently; and eventually we were to come to understand that he also uses methods more subtle than man himself: extra-sensory perception and telepathy. It was as pointless to study one of these methods in isolation, as it would be to try to understand English by studying only the verbs.

We also discovered that each horse expresses itself differently. So we started to compile a dictionary of signs and sounds used by horses, and we found that, apart from a few exceptions, it was impossible to say that a certain sound meant a certain thing. But it was possible within certain limits to say that a horse would convey a certain meaning in one of a defined number of ways. 'Welcome', for example, can be said by a low wicker; it can also be said by a gesture, such as rubbing his nose against you.

On the other hand, the welcome wicker might have a number of meanings as well as 'welcome.' Cork Beg would say 'Welcome' to my wife using his wicker, but the same wicker could mean 'Come here' to his girl friend; or, to me, an instruction to hurry with his feed. He would use exactly the same note on each occasion. It was, we discovered, the context in which the note was used that told you exactly what the horse was saying.

By raising the note of his wicker, we found that the horse could put an imperative into what he was saying. If he got impatient with his current girl friend, for instance, the wicker of 'Darling come here,' would very quickly change to a higher and more urgent note which said 'Get over here immediately you lazy little bitch'. And he did the same to me if I didn't bring him his breakfast straight away in the morning. 'Where is my breakfast,' would change to 'Where is my bloody breakfast you fool, I'm starving.'

The 'welcome' call alone had six imperatives, all of which meant approximately the same thing if used in greeting, but the higher notes used in a different context could also mean, 'Is anybody about?' A similar note would be used by a companion in reply, to say 'I'm here.'

All of this sounds very complicated at first, but once you start understanding your horses, it will be much simpler than it sounds. We also found that when a horse discovered that the messages that he was trying to convey were understood, either by another horse or by man, his range of communication could be extended considerably.

Our researches revealed that there were some thirty or so basic phrases which were used by the domestic horse; but over the course of time we discovered that there were also another seventeen which were used occasionally, or in special situations.

For example a whole series of messages applied to the love play between mare and stallion; and another set of messages were used by the mare in caring for a foal.

Different breeds of horses have slightly different ways of using sounds and signs, and in a large group of mixed horses and ponies, horses of the same breed tend to form smaller groups in a very short time. So though the way of imparting any message does vary from horse to horse, similarities may be seen in horses of the same breed.

In the same way one may trace similarities according to age, or sex – bearing in mind that there are of course three sexes in domestic horses: male, female and gelding.

The horse has, as I have mentioned, eleven different tones of voice. Two of these are made by inhaling: one is a sniff, the other a gentle breathing in. The remaining nine tones are made by exhaling: the snort, the blow through the nostrils, the wicker and the whinny use the nostrils; the neigh and the bell come from the upper nasal region; the squeals come from the nose and mouth; and finally the scream comes from the lung, in a gust of pain, fear, and rage. Each of these eleven tones can be made in a large number of keys, which again help to convey the meaning.

In the wild, the stallion has the greatest vocal range; but the mare has the ability to convey the greatest number of messages.

Among domesticated horses, however, it is a mare owned by a man, or a gelding owned by a woman, that will extend its vocabulary to the greatest degree. In some cases, in the process of understanding and response between man and beast, the vocabulary of the horse can be almost doubled.

In learning to interpret the horse's vocal sounds, the tone, note and delivery are all to be taken into account, and so are the non-verbal messages – the body signs – that accompany the sound. A message such as 'that hurt' for instance, may be communicated in several different forms: by a sharp intake of breath, a wicker, a whinny, a neigh or a scream of pain. Each of these taken by itself may sound like a dozen other messages, but taken with the body signs and the feeling you get from the horse, the meaning will be very plain.

The following story very well illustrates what I mean. Some years ago we had about fifty acres of land about twelve miles from our main farm, on which we ran some odds and ends of ponies and young horses that we weren't doing anything particular with. I would go over once or twice a week to see them, and going over was always a penance as it entailed doing about eight miles on the main Sidmouth to Seaton road which, during the summer, was a hell of roaring cars, stinking petrol, choking exhaust fumes, frustrating traffic jams and frayed tempers. But it was worth it, because once you got there – I always tried to go over in the evening – you found yourself in a valley completely secluded from the rush of the main road. It was like walking into a patch of paradise – I always felt rather like a lost soul who, having had a taste of hell, was finally allowed through the Pearly Gates.

This particular evening as I walked through the gate, the only sounds I could hear were the liquid note of a thrush and the croak of a crow. As I wandered down looking for the ponies through the towering, billowing crowds of bracken, with the sun beating down on my neck, I could almost believe in fairies – especially when I came to clearings in the bracken which had been mowed by the razor edges of a thousand rabbits' teeth.

Eventually after a very short search I found the ponies sheltering under a patch of trees. They were standing like statues, the only movement being the pendulum-like swing of their tails, ticking away the seconds to eternity.

My peace was shattered by the realization that Mousie and her foal were missing. I foresaw a very tedious search through the alder trees down the bottom, and was just turning round for a preliminary search through the bracken when I heard a sharp and imperative whinny from below me. I immediately walked down to where Mousie was standing, in obvious irritation and rage. Mousie was on one side of the bog, and her foal was on the other side of the bog, beyond the next door fence. I slipped a piece of twine over Mousie's neck and led her back down the side of the bog to where I knew there was a weak place in the fence. The foal, neighing in agitation when she saw us going away from her, immediately started to walk along the top of the bank. She fell off. Mousie wickered encouragement to her, the foal got to her feet and cantered down the other side of the fence trying to keep up. Eventually we came to the weak place, and without very much difficulty got the foal through. But now we came to another obstacle. As far as the foal was concerned, it was impossible to walk through six inches of water in the stream. I led Mousie away, Mousie called to the foal to follow, and eventually she summoned up her courage, put in a gigantic leap and cleared the water by at least two feet. Mousie started wickering reassurances to the foal, who shot her head under the milk bar, and took some well-earned nourishment.

As I walked back through the bracken to my car, and the hell of a main road, I realized that Mousie had illustrated for me a whole library of vocal messages. She had used in fact only a small range of whinny and wicker sounds, but her movements, her stance and the situation itself had given them a series of quite specific meanings, clear as much to me as to the foal itself. So my journey had been very much worth while.

As well as the forty-seven basic messages we were eventually able to identify through our researches, we discovered there were also fifty-four sub-messages. Some of these we assumed to be natural to horses in the wild, others not, but we found that even a wild horse fresh from the hills would learn the 'domesticated' vocabulary very quickly, usually from other horses.

Our best teacher without doubt was Cork Beg, who had the most extensive vocabulary of any horse we've ever had. We very quickly discovered that, as he extended his own vocabulary, he was teaching other horses as well, and we ran a series of trials over the eighteen years we had him to see how quickly he could teach other horses basic phrases.

We would put a wild and untouched pony in with Cork Beg at feeding time, for instance. Cork Beg would ask for food, and in a very short time his young companion would be whinnying in imitation. Then, when segregated again, the colt would ask for food when he was hungry. Of a hundred and twenty-two cases only three had not learned to ask for food within seven days.

All these experiments, our experience in communicating with horses and the dictionary we compiled of horse language, are treated at length in my book *Talking with Horses*. Here I propose only to remind the reader of the basic principles of horse communication, because no one can begin to study horse psychology without first learning to read the messages his animal is sending.

Anyone wishing to understand his horse should start by learning to observe the whole complex of body movements – some of them the mere flick of a muscle – with which the horse signals his messages. Horses' sign language is far more easily understood than their vocal messages, partly because the signs follow a far more definite pattern. Each sign tends to have a consistent meaning. Aggressive movements for instance are easy to interpret. The sign may be a mere flicking of the skin, or the relaxation of a set of muscles, but the message is there for anyone to see. Most horsemen anyway understand most of these signs, and all vets use the sign language when diagnosing a sick or an injured horse. In conveying messages the ears are nearly always used, but they mean far more than most people realize. Everyone knows that the ears flat back mean 'I'm going to buck.' The ears half back on the other hand simply mean, 'I'm relaxed,' or, if you have the habit of talking to your horses when you are riding as I have, 'I'm listening to the tone of your voice'. In some cases ear movements have a distinct meaning in themselves, and in others they are only part of a whole message being conveyed by body movements, voice and other means simultaneously. The neck, tail, legs, skin and all the muscles are used to give signs. But remember that interpretation can be learnt only by being patient, and observing the horse quietly.

When we came to trying to talk back to the horse, of course, we could not reproduce his signs exactly, but we could use our own bodies to convey feelings: comfort, encouragement, reproach. We found that we could use our arms to comfort, as the horse uses his neck. And our hands and fingers could make similar caressing movements to his head and nose: the feeling he got when being caressed by the tip of our fingers was very similar to the feeling he got when being caressed by the nose of another horse. In exactly the same way a slap of the hand gave a sting like that of a nip from an outraged companion.

The arrival of the Pooka, a fourteen-two three-year-old Skewbald gelding, illustrated how both signs and sounds could be put to use in horse psychology. The Pooka kicked, and kicked badly at anyone who went near him. His owner and everyone else was terrified with him. So when he arrived we turned him straight out with Cork Beg, Honesty and Wolsey. Cork Beg jogged over to investigate him. As soon as Cork Beg got near enough to him, the Pooka whipped around and lashed out. Cork Beg, as boss of the herd, wasn't having this. He quickly switched ends so that his well shod heels were pointing towards Pooka, and belted hell out of him. Pooka returned to the corner. Cork Beg followed and again kicked the living daylights out of him. Ten seconds later, before I could intervene, Cork Beg trotted away, leaving Pooka cowering in terror in the ditch. Ten minutes later the Pooka very slowly and hesitantly edged towards the other three horses. When he got to within about five yards of them, Honesty, who was normally extremely mild and inoffensive, turned her head, put her ears back and raised one leg. The Pooka retreated in terror. All ideas of being the big bumptious bully had disappeared in the ten seconds' treatment meted out to him by Cork Beg.

I noted that instant and severe retribution had made an immediate change in Pooka's whole attitude. When he entered the field his one desire had been to dominate the whole group, and yet thirty seconds later, his one idea was not to offend anyone. And he even seemed quite happy with his new humbled status in the herd, though his humility receded slightly over the next day or two as his natural youth and exuberance once more asserted themselves.

This example of how the desires and habits of a horse could be changed by using the correct method of communication was not lost on me, so when I got the Pooka in two or three days later to start work on him, and he swung round and lashed out at me, I put my new knowledge to good use. I dodged his kick with a nifty piece of footwork which brought me at right angles to him, and as I landed, brought one foot back and landed the toe of my boot in his midriff. The Pooka was turned into a pillar of salt, so great was his surprise. So to drive the message home I followed my left boot with my right boot. This was too much for the Pooka, who shrivelled up in a corner like a de-flated balloon. I stood still for two or three seconds, and then started talking to him quietly, walking towards him. He shrank to an even smaller size, but allowed me to get a hand on him to touch him, and then slowly, I worked my fingers round, still talking to him gently. He gradually began to reflate, until he was standing normally, though very tense. Another ten minutes' talking and gentle rhythmic movement of my fingers on his skin brought him into a relaxed and happy state.

Having got to this point, I left him alone, and went and got him something to eat. As I came in with the bucket he made a rush at the doorway. I clouted him smartly across the nose, and he retreated to his corner and stared at me. This form of treatment was completely new to him. He had been shouted at, he'd been hit before for kicking people but no one had ever slapped him across the nose and then walked over and made a fuss of him because he had done the right thing. And I could see that the communication was getting through to him very quickly. At the same time his attitude to human beings and life was being altered. He was learning that when he did the wrong thing he was instantly punished, but when he did the right thing he was made a fuss of.

The more we studied how the horses were communicating with each other and with us, however, the more we came to realize that there was more to communication than signs and sounds. We became convinced that the horses were sensing our moods and feelings and anticipating our wishes. I began to read around the subject, and my reading reinforced my suspicion that some form of communication other than sounds and signs was at work. Although nothing I read treated the subject scientifically or even explicitly, all the books on horses seemed to contain phrases like 'put your heart over a fence and your horse will follow.' We called this undefined factor in communication Extra-Sensory Perception. We knew that the fact that our horses seemed instinctively to know our moods could in part be explained by what they could see and hear, but there was more to it than this. To discover the real nature of this instinctive knowledge, we ran over the next ten years a series of experiments with pairs of horses whom we knew to be friends – what we call empathic pairs.

An empathic pair is simply two horses which are mentally and emotionally close to each other. Such horses may find themselves automatically in tune with each other from the first time they meet: these will probably be of the same breed and type. Or alternatively they may become mentally in tune with each other through close and constant companionship. A truly empathic pair is a pair of horses who literally think as one. From among the forty or fifty horses we were handling each year, over a period of five years we selected eleven pairs in all, of which we found eight pairs suitable for our experiments.

These experiments I have described in detail in *Talking with Horses*, and I shall only summarize them here. But what we learnt in these experiments about the extraordinary mental capabilities of the horse was fundamental to our future work on horse psychology.

Five experiments were involved, which we ran over a period of three days. We carried out each experiment three times, varying the horses that we were working with.

In the first experiment, the two horses were placed in separate stalls, well out of sight and hearing of each other. One of each pair was then fed in a plastic container. For us to record a positive reaction his empathic pair had at the same time to indicate that he wanted food. To make quite sure there was no question of habit coming into the experiments, the horses were not fed at the same time every day, nor were they fed at their regular feeding times. In twenty-one out of the twenty-four tests we had a positive response, which was better than we had dared hope. That is to say, on twenty-one out of the twenty-four occasions, when we were feeding one horse, the second horse, even though he couldn't see or hear us in any way, knew that we were feeding his empathic pair and demanded food.

In the second experiment, one of each pair was taken out of the yard into a field and excited by cantering, jumping, and generally getting him hotted up. For this experiment the horse pair was always in a loose box where he couldn't see his companion leaving the yard. A positive result was recorded if the horse in the loose box became excited.

Experiment three was a more or less complete failure, because the positive results left too much room for human error. It involved trying to calm an excited horse by gentling – caressing and calming by voice – not him but his companion. The difficulty lay in deciding how long it would have taken the horse to relax *without* the gentling of his pair.

But the fourth experiment was quite simple. I would talk to and make a fuss of one of the pair, usually the one I liked the least, and a positive result was recorded if the other, well out of sight and hearing, showed signs of jealousy: that is if it became unsettled and disturbed.

The fifth experiment was rather an unpleasant one and I don't think I would like to repeat it. It involved frightening one of the horses. But since one of the most basic emotions in an animal is fear, I felt that it was extremely important to prove that fear as well as excitement, jealousy, and the desire for food could be conveyed by Extra-Sensory Perception. In this case I frightened the horse by rushing toward him, clenching my fist, and chasing him round and round the box until he was extremely nervous. A positive result was recorded if his companion became nervous too. This happened in sixteen out of the twenty-four cases.

Out of the one hundred and nineteen experiments we carried out, we had positive results in eighty-one cases, a marginal result in twelve more, and a possible result in eleven cases, which gave us a definite overall success rate of 67.5 percent: well above the rate that could be predicted by pure chance. We had to conclude that some extra-sensory form of communication was indeed being used.

A point of interest that arose from this series of experiments was that we found that the horses seemed to be able to switch from one thought wave-length to another. That is, some horses who have one natural thought-pattern, according to their breed and upbringing, learnt to communicate with horses of quite different breed and thought-pattern after a long period of close companionship.

So we ran another series of experiments to test these thought-patterns. We chose four horses, each of which we knew had communication with at least one other horse in the group. For convenience we will call them horses A, B, C and D.

We discovered that if we fed horse A, horses B, C and D all indicated a desire for food. If we fed horse A, having removed horse B to some distance away, horses C and D did NOT ask for food. Similarly if we fed horse A whilst horse B was present, and horse C was absent, horse B would ask for food but horse D would not. If we fed horse D without horse C being present, neither horses B nor A would ask for food. Therefore we were able to conclude that

Horse A had communication with horse B.
" B " " " " A & C.
" C " " " " B & D.
" D " " " " C, and not with any of
the other horses.

It would seem therefore that some horses were able to communicate only with horses of a similar thought-pattern to their own, while others – in this case horses B and C, could communicate with horses of different patterns.

We also discovered that Extra-Sensory Perception thought-patterns are not a static thing; by companionship and association horses could and did change their thought-patterns over a period of time.

This concept of thought-patterns helped to explain why a horse can get on well with one horse and not with another. And we discovered that our ability to get through to any horse was entirely dependent on our ability to think on the same wavelength, that is to learn his pattern of thought.

I discovered early on, for example, that I could get through to thoroughbreds without any difficulties. But I had a great deal of difficulty in establishing any rapport with small ponies. Over the years I have developed an ability to switch wave-lengths from one horse to another, but this took a lot of work and a lot of practice.

Extra-Sensory Perception, it emerged from our work eventually, apparently has four different functions, which may be used separately or possibly together.

The first is to convey mood: friendly or hostile, peaceful or excited.

The second is to convey emotion, such as anger or love.

The third is to convey needs, such as hunger and thirst.

And fourth, these three functions together enable the horse also to convey limited ideas: such as 'here is good grass', 'let's go away' or 'I'm hungry'. 'I'm hungry' or 'Here is good grass' would come through to another horse simply as hunger, and hunger diminished, and 'I'm frightened, let's run away', would come through as fear, and fear diminished.

We realized of course in all our work on communication that the horse is of comparatively limited intellect: we thought of it in human terms as that of a child of about eight, though a stupid horse could have the mental capacity of a dull seven-year-old and a clever horse could have the ability of an intelligent nine-year-old. And we very quickly learnt that the intelligent ones were the most difficult horses, and often unrideable if they had been mishandled. But these were the horses that I preferred, since they extended my ability to the limit.

My interest in Extra-Sensory Perception, and the work we did on it, was first triggered off by the purchase of an emaciated and neglected eight-year-old gelding named Weeping Roger. This purchase nearly led to the breakdown of our marriage. I can never resist buying an emaciated, broken-down old thoroughbred, I've got a spiritual kinship with them; but emaciated and broken-down old thoroughbreds cost a fortune to feed, and they usually mean trouble, so Leslie when she sees me after one is likely to cut up very rough indeed. But on this occasion I was a little bit too quick for her, and I bought Weeping Roger.

When I began to exercise Roger, I found that all I had to do was get on his back, slip my hands into my pockets (it was winter, and cold) and think where I wanted to go, and the pace I wanted him to go at. I could direct and control him entirely by thinking what I wanted to do next. Now how much this was due to un-conscious signals I was giving him, and how much to Roger's ability to interpret *my* thought-patterns, I can't definitely know. The only thing I know is that by working on the subject consciously I could control him. Thinking I was on to a good thing, I thought I would try exactly the same thing on Wolsey.

So the following morning I got on to Wolsey, and since it was particularly cold, jammed my hands in my trouser pockets and started off. All went well for the first fifty yards. Then Wolsey, instead of walking as I wanted him to, started trotting. So with great concentration, I relaxed my body to make Wolsey relax, and thought about the muscular movements of the walk. To no avail. Wolsey's trot quickened, very shortly became a canter, and then a hard gallop. With me still thinking hard about walking, we proceeded up the track until Wolsey, finding his head free, decided to put it between his knees, throw four colossal bucks and stop suddenly to watch with great satisfaction as I turned three very neat somersaults in the air and landed on my back-side. Rubbing the painful bruise left by a large stone on my posterior, I walked back down to the yard to recapture Wolsey, who had preceded me there at the rate of knots. This gave me adequate time to realize that you cannot control every horse by Extra-Sensory Perception.

So it was a question of back to the drawing board. By pains-taking study we discovered that the limitations on the use of Extra-Sensory Perception as a means of control are as follows:

a) when you are using it the horse is entirely free to do what he wants;

b) its effectiveness is limited by your own ability to get through to that particular horse; and

c) in exactly the same way as when you are trying to control or understand a horse using signs and sounds, you have to see any single aspect of communication as only part of the whole pattern of language, and not rely on only one part of the whole.

In other words, it is impossible to communicate with the horse successfully using only signs and sounds, and it is just as impossible to communicate with a horse using Extra-Sensory Perception without using signs and sounds as well.

Our work on Extra-Sensory Perception led to the discovery of a fourth method of communication, used comparatively rarely but important all the same. We discovered between 1958 and 1964 that whole mental pictures may be transmitted from one animal to another: that horses can and do have the ability to communicate by telepathy. The two animals do not necessarily have to be of the same species, but they usually are. And, we found that we could use the horse's ability to 'read' telepathic messages in our riding by 'transmitting' mental pictures ourselves, mainly of where we wanted the horse to go. Also, when we came to an object the horse was likely to shy at, we discovered that by gazing intently at the object we could make the horse see it for what it was, a stone or a twig, not a tiger about to spring. So he didn't shy.

Early in 1958 we had a grey gelding called Iron Side sent down to us from Ascot. He was said to be unrideable because of his shying: he would refuse to pass quite simple objects, and shy into the path of oncoming traffic, which made him extremely dangerous to ride.

I guessed from the beginning that part of the trouble was in the weakness of his owner, but first I had him checked for defective vision. The vet examined his eyesight, and after exhaustive tests he decided that his vision was absolutely normal; but that due to the position of his eyes, and his very prominent cheek bones, he wasn't seeing objects behind and below him as well as a horse normally does. When loose, this didn't matter because he was constantly turning his head, but when being ridden on a tight rein he would have difficulty. Since his owner was so nervous about his shying, she was keeping him on an extremely tight rein, which of course would make him very nervous in turn.

I set out to cure this, first by riding him on a very slack rein and making him stop, look, and walk up to any object he shied at. Then I discovered that if I rode him on a slack rein and at the same time gazed intently at any likely object myself, he didn't seem to need to shy at all. And after about a fortnight riding him like this, including four hard days' hunting, he became quiet and sensible and almost completely stopped shying.

We also found that horses used telepathy among themselves to direct other horses to food and water, especially over distances when they were out of earshot and out of sight of each other; or to split the herd in time of danger.

To test our telepathy theory we devised what we called the Kit-e-Kat experiment, inspired by the television advertisements starring the white cat, Arthur. Cork Beg was offered two containers of food, and I had to try to direct him to the one out of which I wanted him to eat, using nothing but telepathy. There was considerable preparation and training before we could start, but after a fortnight's training we ran a series of twelve experiments, and in all twelve of them he chose the container to which I had directed him.

Cork Beg was a very easy subject, because he wanted to please. But nevertheless I had to learn a very intense form of concentration: the picture of the feed laying in the bottom of the bucket had to be very vivid in my mind's eye. Above all, such an experiment depends on complete communication between man and horse.

Also, over ten years, we developed the habit of recording telepathic communication whenever it seemed to have occurred. When we thought we had telepathic communication with one of our horses or with each other, we made a note of what had happened, and, most important of all, recorded the time that it had happened. In the end we had thirty or forty proven cases of telepathy: three recorded occurrences, with exact times, were across distances of over eighteen miles, and one instance was over two hundred and forty miles, although we were unable to count this as a verified account because there was no recording of the exact time, for our definition of verified telepathic communication required that the time be recorded within a quarter of an hour, and that the picture received must be recorded in writing at the time it was received.

It is easy to identify what animal you are receiving the message from, since he won't be in the picture you are receiving. So if for example I received a telepathic communication from Cork Beg, I would know I was receiving it from Cork Beg and not from Iantella, if Iantella was in the picture and Cork Beg was not.

Telepathy is the most difficult form of communication to learn, though since it is used only to a very limited extent, the skill is not essential to the handling of horses.

But our work on communication was only part of our continuing work on Horse Psychology. We wanted really to understand what made our horses tick.

3: *First Lessons in Horse Behaviour*

As we began better to understand what our horses were saying to us, and to interpret it, we also began to see that we could not generalize about horses in general from the individual behaviour of any horse.

We could see for example that the things that excited Cork Beg left Wolsey completely cold, and vice-versa. Cork Beg was a very shy feeder. He'd pick a mouthful of food out of his basin, then walk over to the door and have a look to see what was going on outside. Then he might or might not go back and have another mouthful. Whereas Wolsey's whole life revolved around his belly: the only real interest he had in life, other than hunting, was to see how much he could stuff into his mouth, and how quickly. So if we wanted Wolsey to do something in particular, such as allow himself to be loaded on a lorry, we had only to rattle a bucket of nuts, and Wolsey would be ready to follow you through the gates of hell to get at them. But since Cork Beg wasn't interested in food at all it was no incentive to him to try and tempt him with a bucket of nuts, and we had to invent subtler encouragements.

The two horses' likes and dislikes were as different as they were different physically; and if their likes and dislikes were different it seemed probable that their psychological patterns would be different too.

We could not observe thought-patterns. But we could observe the way such patterns were expressed in behaviour, so we set out to study horse behaviour. Above all we were interested in the horses' reactions to us, and to our actions. But we started by studying the horses' reactions to each other. The first task was to watch our own horses, very carefully, and with open minds. One of the first things we observed was that whilst two friends

42

would caress each other with their noses, and scratch each other with their teeth, they never patted each other. The nearest thing to a pat that one horse gave another was a bite or a kick. So we concluded that if we patted a young or a nervous horse, the horse would think that we were punishing it for something. We also saw that when a strange horse approached another, he would sniff, or blow through his nostrils at it. And that when any horse was frightened by something, it would go into the main bunch and seek bodily contact and reassurance. A mare too would reassure a frightened foal by nuzzling it. And we imitated these actions as best we could with our own bodies.

Soon we found that we were having far less trouble with difficult and nervous horses. One of our first tests came when my friend, Henry Squires of Bower Hinton Martock, brought me two unbroken colts of about fifteen-two hands, straight off Sedgemoor. They were turned into the yard, but I managed to separate them into two adjoining loose boxes with comparative ease, simply by taking Wolsey into the yard, leading him into the first of the loose boxes and driving the colts in after him. Then we took Wolsey out, and the colts of course tried to shoot out too. We let one back into the yard and quickly shut the door on the other. Then Wolsey was taken into the adjoining loose box, the second colt followed him, and was shut in in turn.

I started working with the first colt, a grey gelding that we called Tinsel. He was very wild and very nervous. His only experience of man had been being caught for castration in the spring, so it was hardly surprising.

Previously our method had been to get a halter on to the colt somehow, and leave him tied up for a while to fight the halter. Then I'd simply get on his back until he bucked himself out. Whilst this was very exciting, I was absolutely certain it wasn't the best way to quieten a nervous horse. So putting my new observation into practice, this time I just walked into the loose box and shut the door. Tinsel made a very creditable attempt at climbing up the walls, but there was no escape. So he stood in the far corner and shivered. I just blew at him, and was very agreeably surprised to see how quickly he settled down. Slowly, one inch at a time, I eased myself towards the middle of the loose box. Each time I moved, he froze like a statue ready for flight. But after about half an hour I managed to get right up to him. As chance would have it, I came not to his head but to the middle of his body and slowly and very tentatively stretched out my hand. As I touched his coat with my fingers, it was as if he had been branded with a red hot iron: he exploded into a frenzy of belting around the box. I just stood still until he came to rest again. And again I edged into him, and touched him with my fingers. This time, apart from trying to disappear through the wall of the box, he didn't move. Slowly and gently I moved my fingers round until I got the whole of my hand, and then the whole of my body up against him. After about five minutes of this treatment he relaxed completely.

Having succeeded beyond my wildest dreams, I left him for the day. I came back to him early the following morning however, and by lunch time the following day I had a halter on him without any battle at all. Very quickly he came to look upon me as an extremely friendly animal.

His companion Russet, whilst even more nervous to begin with, relaxed quicker still, and I had him riding quite quietly within about three days.

Having demonstrated to my own satisfaction the effective application of horse psychology, I went back to my work on equine behaviour with renewed zest.

I found that each piece of work was falling into three stages. First I would observe the behaviour of the horses among themselves in the field, or the response of a horse to some action of mine, and make a note of what I saw. Then I would have to think about it, to deduce what motivation might lie behind the behaviour I had observed. And having made my deduction, I would carry out an experiment to see whether I could reproduce that behaviour with other horses, in the same way.

I could see, for example, that the horses got excited if I blew the hunting horn. Now it didn't take very much intelligence to guess that it was not only my accomplishment as a musician that was sending the horses into ecstasies, but the association of the sound of the horn with the excitement of the hunt. I could verify this in two ways. First I played a variety of musical instruments to see whether the horses were interested in them – which of course they were not. Then I blew the hunting horn to horses that had no experience of hunting whatever. Again there was no response. I then felt justified in concluding that it was the association with the hunt that excited the horses when I blew the hunting horn.

One of the aspects of horse behaviour that had always interested us was the question of dominance within the herd. We observed over some ten years that certain horses, irrespective of their size, would take over the leadership of the herd, while other horses, no matter what group of horses you put them with, would take a subservient position. We also found that horses gravitated naturally to one of four groups within the herd: the boss group, the upper middle group, the lower middle group or the bottom group.

Then we had a little bit of time on our hands, and decided to run a series of tests or trials on herd behaviour. We split the main herd into three separate groups, and as each new horse arrived we would put him in with one of these groups. After about seven days we would note the position he had assumed within the herd. Then we would remove him from herd A, and put him into herd B, again note the position he assumed in that herd, and repeat the process in herd C.

Herd A was a group of seven registered Welsh Cobs, all similarly bred and from the same farm.

Herd B was a mixed group of thirteen-two and fourteen-two ponies.

And herd C was again a mixed group, of two-year-olds, three-year-olds and twelve-twos.

We found our earlier observations completely verified: it didn't matter which group the new horse entered – and as a complete stranger he would not know the other horses of course – he automatically took the same position every time. If he was a top echelon horse, he went into the top group of the herd. If he was a subservient horse he'd go to the tail of the herd. And if he belonged to one of the middle groups, he would go there.

A classical example of this behaviour was Star Light. Star Light was a twelve-two stallion which I had bought in Llanbyther. We brought him home and had him castrated the next day. I knew that after castration he would make an extremely high quality gelding.

We put him in herd C first. And after he had demolished the two leaders of that herd without any difficulty whatever, we took him out and put him straight in amongst the Welsh Cobs. Every one of the Welsh Cobs was well over fourteen-one, and they were all extremely strong, rumbustious geldings. Rostellan, who was the boss of the herd at the time, trotted over with his brother Red to investigate the intruder. Star Light just stood and watched the approach of these two seasoned campaigners. They came one from either side of him, so that whichever way he turned one of them could clobber him. Star Light just watched, and I watched Star Light. Rostellan trotted up towards his head, whilst Red circled slightly to one side so that he could put two crafty heels into Star Light's ribs. Star Light let them get just close enough, then he pivoted like a ballet dancer on his front feet and planted two hoofs hard into Rostellan's chest. As his feet touched the ground, he launched himself with his teeth and front feet straight at the unsuspecting Red, caught him with both feet, gripped his neck with his teeth, and wrenched, ending up with a mouthful of skin and hair. Red fled, with Star Light in hot pursuit. Red made a circle of the field, but as they came back past Rostellan, Star Light put the brakes on and Rostellan, who had been observing this scene, suddenly found that he was the one at the receiving end of Star Light's fury. He too disappeared for the horizon. Star Light did two circuits of the field, with head and tail up, snorting in triumph, after which he proceeded to whip the rest of the herd into a suitable state of submission.

Pound for pound he was the equivalent to a fly-weight compared with two heavy-weights, but his aggressiveness and mental dominance had far outweighed any disadvantage of weight and size.

We did another experiment on the emotional influence of one horse on another. The only thing necessary to carry out this experiment was time and patience. We repeated it time and time again with various horses, but the most clearcut case was that of Merlin and Chance. Merlin was extremely placid, easy going and rather lazy, whereas Chance was excitable and very nervous. Over a period of five months we kept them in close contact together, in adjoining loose boxes in the stable and working together the whole time. At the end of the five months the behaviour change in Chance was extremely marked: he had steadied down considerably, he would walk extremely well – before he had danced and jogged along all the time – and his jumping had become controlled where previously he had gone tearing madly into his fences. Then Merlin went back to his owner. Chance began to revert to his earlier behaviour, and if anything his excitability and nervousness became worse than before he had come under Merlin's influence.

These are just two very minor examples of what might be called observational research and experiment. But they illustrate the type of work that can be done quite simply by anyone with enough patience and care, who wants to understand the behaviour of horses. One rule, however, must be remembered: you can only prove one thing at a time.

If, for instance, your horse is sleepy and dull and you suspect he is suffering from mineral deficiency, it is no use adding oats *and* mineral supplement to his diet, because even if he regains his alertness you will never know whether it was the oats, or the minerals, or both that did the trick.

Similarly, if your horse won't jump for you, and someone else gets on carrying a stick and he then jumps, you don't know whether he is jumping because of the change of rider, or because of the stick. You must change only one factor at a time.

Having identified a factor – say a change in the way you ride him – that affects the behaviour of a particular horse, you can then try the same change with other horses, and thus establish whether your discovery applies to horses in general, or simply to one special horse.

I had been keen for some time to study the effects that changes in environment and handling could have on the performance of a horse, so when a friend asked me to buy a thoroughbred two-year-old for him at Newmarket, to run his pony mares, I persuaded my very reluctant Bank manager to allow me to purchase a horse for myself at the same time.

So one November Sunday Leslie and I departed for the wild and dangerous world of Newmarket. We arrived there on the Sunday night, and at half-past-eight on the Monday morning, determined not to miss a minute of it, we arrived at the Sale Yard. For the next hour we admired and examined the cream of the racing industry.

I always like buying horses at Newmarket. With a limited pocket like my own, when buying for myself, I can only afford to buy rubbish at a sale. But the advantage of Newmarket is that you get a much better class of rubbish there than anywhere else.

The first two or three lots in were thoroughbred two-year-old weeds, of no pedigree or racing distinction, and they were all led out unsold. But lot seven was a different sort of horse altogether: a fifteen-three chestnut by Eudaemon with a lot of bone, substance and quality. Whilst he had no racing pedigree, he was the perfect horse for a crossing stallion, so I purchased him for my friend, for a very small sum.

The next three lots again were of no interest to me, but lot eleven was the horse I wanted. He had an excellent pedigree, and had won as a two-year-old, then over the next three or four years had won three races and been placed seven times. Then as a six-year-old he had just packed it in and had never done a thing since, which is to say he hadn't troubled the judge: the judge must have had considerable difficulty in seeing him in the far distance when the rest of the field had passed the winning post. And indeed when he came into the ring, with his big head half way down between his knees, he was the picture of complete dejection. Life held nothing for him now, and the sale ring at Newmarket was just another piece of degradation in a long and tedious life.

Without any difficulty I bought him for a maiden bid of fifty quid, and having done my business I left to get home to Wales in time to do the milking that night.

The two horses arrived in the yard on the Sunday morning, and before they had been unloaded from the trailer, the purchaser of the two-year-old arrived. He asked how much? I told him what I wanted for the horse, and he said 'I'll have him', and this before he had seen more than the colour of its tail.

We transferred Broken Promise to Stan Williams' trailer, and then unloaded Argonaut. Argonaut walked into the yard, looked round, put his head back to its customary place between his knees, and trailed slowly into the stable.

Over the next three months we made strenuous efforts to penetrate Argonaut's barrier of sullen dejection and boredom with everything.

The first thing I noticed was that although he was eating plenty of food, he wasn't looking for his breakfast with any zest, so for a week or ten days I cut back his feed to practically nothing: just two or three pounds of corn three times a day. As soon as his belly was being affected, Argonaut started to take more interest, and soon enough, when I went out with his feed in the morning, he was screaming for it and telling me that I was starving him.

The next thing was to get him to take an interest in his work. So instead of doing normal exercise, I used him for shepherding, which meant not only that he had the interest of watching the dog working the sheep, he also had to shepherd the sheep himself. And very quickly, if a sheep broke, he was spinning round and going flat out after it. Whilst this wasn't very good for the sheep, it was extremely good for Argonaut.

And to replace his racing gallops and schooling over fences, I took him out hunting.

It happened at this time that in one of our best pieces of country we had a semi-tame fox. He used to live in the gorse on the other side of the road from the house by day, and during cold wet nights he'd sleep in the hay shed and he'd steal any bits of bone that the sheep dog had left behind. We always knew him because when he was a cub he had been a bit slow going out of the yard one morning, and as he jumped the fence my bull terrier made a leap and caught hold of his tail. They had a tug of war, something had to give, so the fox's tail parted in the middle, leaving him with an abbreviated brush about three inches long. After that we could always identify him. And from then on we christened him the bob tail fox, commonly known as Bob.

Bob was a great womanizer. He roamed all over the country, and two or three times a season, especially during the mating season, while we were out hunting, we'd put Bob up and he'd head straight for home.

On one of our first days hunting, Argonaut was not showing much interest. He performed adequately, but no more. There was no heart in his jumping or his galloping, until suddenly the hounds put Bob up out of the cover just above Llanybyther, and away we went. We had a couple of little fly fences, and with my wife on Cork Beg and myself on Argonaut, we took them stride for stride. And then Bob swung slightly to the left, and we had a mile straight across a whole farm with nothing to stop us. Two or three banks in the middle, and Argonaut really stretched out and Cork Beg stretched out with him. At the far end of this was a gate on to the road. Argonaut was determined that he was going to get to it first, so he sprinted a little bit and flew the gate, landing on the verge, almost slipping as he turned on the road.

We had about three quarters of a mile on the verge of a piece of forestry land and as we came to the bottom of it we could see hounds streaming up past home and into the gorse. They hunted the fox at the top end of the gorse for about ten minutes. Then as we came to the gate of the yard we saw Bob coming down on top of the bank, completely unruffled. He turned along the bottom of the gorse by the road, ran up a big gorse bush and proceeded to jump from one gorse bush to the next, until he disappeared from view.

Hounds came down the bank about a hundred yards behind him, swung along the bottom and were completely baffled by Bob's trick. I put Argonaut in and got out another horse to take the hounds back to the Huntsman, whom we met coming up the road about half a mile away. We handed over the hounds and went back to the yard to make sure Argonaut was quite comfortable. And he was walking around and around his box to relieve his pent-up excitement. From that day on he was a changed character.

Since I had done so well out of my expedition to Newmarket, my Bank manager didn't need much persuading to allow me to go back to the sales to buy another horse to help restore the Blake family fortunes.

Unfortunately on my second visit, horses were much more expensive and I couldn't see anything I wanted at a price that I could afford. So at the end of the first day I decided to stay overnight, and try again the following morning.

In the bar of the hotel after dinner I was having a well needed restorative, when I got chatting to someone else who was similarly employed. We were both looking for the same sort of horse, and we both had been frustrated by the prices.

I happened to mention to him that I had an eight-year-old for sale with a bit of form about him and who was quite a fair hunter, and before much ado we had concluded the deal at five hundred on condition that he could have the horse on a fortnight's trial. So we both turned to go to bed.

As we reached the door of the bar, he said 'By the way, what's the name of this horse?' And I told him 'Argonaut.' He stopped. 'Good God' he said. And I said, 'Why, what's the matter?' He said 'I brought Argonaut down here and sold him six weeks ago for fifty quid.' So we went back to the bar for something to calm our shattered nerves.

It turned out he had bought him as a five-year-old, and done very well with him that season, but never again. Three years later, in despair, he had brought him down to Newmarket for what he could fetch.

When I got home I continued my treatment of Argonaut. I had him sufficiently fit and happy to run him point to point at the first of the season, but he wasn't fully wound up and was beaten on the run in. I took him home and put in a bit more work on him. The next meeting being my local hunt meeting, I started the day off quite nicely, winning the hunt race by a street. Then I had what I always think to be the worst time in racing: a long hour before a race you think you stand a pretty good chance of winning. I just sat in the jockeys' tent visualizing all the things that could go wrong, and all the mistakes I could make which would make me look an even bigger fool than usual. I saddled Argonaut, and he boosted my sagging confidence because he was as fit and as well as he could possibly be. He had his head and his tail up and was really ready to go. Then came the setback: when I got back to the jockeys tent, I was told that the bookies had made him favourite. Now if the bookies make you favourite and you win, nobody gives you any credit; and if you don't win everyone who has backed you goes round telling everyone else that you shouldn't be allowed to ride a donkey on the sands, let alone a racehorse. But, I reasoned, after nearly twenty-one years of riding, I had surely ceased to worry about what people said about my abilities as a jockey.

And then finally one of the stewards' assistants came in and said 'Jockeys out', and the seven of us trooped out, making cheerful noises to each other to hide the fact that our hearts were in our boots and there was a dirty great cavity where our bellies should be. But this is normal to anyone riding a race. I tightened Argonaut's girth and vaulted into the saddle – one of the disadvantages of being the oldest jockey riding is that you have got to prove to the crowd that you are more agile than anyone else, so I do this by vaulting on myself instead of having a leg up. And down to the start.

As an old campaigner I got in on the inside, tight to the starter so that he couldn't see me, and managed to get a flying start. I led by about two lengths into the first fence. Argonaut stood back and rocketed over, and proceeded to do the same with every fence afterwards, never making a mistake, always standing well back and gaining ground in the air. And the further he went the more he was enjoying himself. I didn't see another horse until I came to the second last fence, when the second favourite, May Flower, came up on my side. We flew the fence side by side, landing neck and neck, and drove for the last fence, both of us riding for our lives. As we came into it I thought Argonaut had made a mistake. He took off a stride early, and I thought we had had it. But not a bit. He had put in an extra large jump, and we landed a length in front of May Flower. As we went up the straight, every pounding stride he took carried him just that little bit further in front. We pulled up having won by two lengths, and danced back to the unsaddling enclosure.

As we went in to the paddock, someone roused a ragged cheer, which was all Argonaut needed. He put in two colossal bucks from sheer *joie de vivre*, nearly getting me off.

Argonaut won another race that season, and he was placed every other time he ran. We also discovered he wasn't really a three-mile horse, because he didn't enjoy his racing unless he led from start to finish, and three miles, carrying twelve-seven, was that little bit too far for him. The one race that I tried him coming from behind was the only time that he wasn't in the first three (we finished fourth, with Argonaut putting in a very pedestrian effort). And since he did not enjoy racing unless he was in front, I let him bowl along the way he wanted to, because I knew if he stopped enjoying racing again I would never get him to do anything.

The story of Argonaut shows how, unless you have a horse full of joy and enthusiasm, he won't win a race. And indeed in any form of riding you are restricted by two things: first the horse's physical ability – that is the maximum he can attain with his body when he is fully fit – and second his mental fitness, for when you have a horse fit mentally he will use the absolute limits of his physical ability.

One of the things that continually amazes me is how, in buying a horse, people will pay great respect to the physical make-up of the horse, and give detailed attention to the various points of confirmation, but they take no notice whatsoever of the mental make-up of the horse – which is equally important. Parents buying a pony for their child will be influenced by its colour, and its show points, forgetting that colour and show points have no relevance whatever to its suitability as a children's pony. Dozens and dozens of letters are written to the horse papers about the evils of breeding from sub-standard ponies, yet these may be the very ponies that have the kindness and mental stability that's essential to make a good children's pony. The beautiful show ponies, stallions and mares are often much too excitable for a small child to ride.

It must be remembered too that needs of nutrition and handling will vary from horse to horse. Mental states in the horse can very often be affected by feeding: under-feeding will make a horse much lazier and easier to handle, whilst overfeeding, and underwork, can make him extremely excitable. These things are well known. But it is also true that an imbalance can upset a horse mentally.

So in looking at the psychology of any particular horse, it is essential to make sure that the feeding for that particular horse is correct – always remembering that what is correct for one horse will not necessarily be correct for another. This is particularly important during the period of training, because deficiency of protein in the diet during the time of learning, particularly in infancy (it must of course be remembered that a horse is learning from the time it is born) will retard his learning ability.

This has been experimentally proved with rats. I've done no work myself with horses on this, and I don't know of anyone who has, but a series of trials were carried out with twenty rats on a high protein diet, twenty on a normal diet, and twenty on a diet deficient in protein. And it was discovered that the group of rats on the normal diet took twenty percent less time to learn how to negotiate a maze than those on the high protein diet, who themselves learned how to negotiate the maze twice as quickly as the rats on a deficiency of protein.

Similar tests have been done on other animals, so it is probable that the same principle is true for horses. Great attention in teaching horses must therefore be paid to correct diet, which should be neither too high nor too low in protein, and balanced in mineral intake. A horse that seems to be stupid, awkward, or bloody-minded may simply be suffering from a food deficiency.

It is also true that the character and ability of the person handling a horse can considerably affect its performance. Constant weakness in handling from birth, for example, can make a horse unmanageable as a three- or four-year-old, while too much severity and brutality can terrify a horse so much that he becomes mentally unstable.

The worst example of this that we have had was a horse called Potty. He was called Potty because he was completely mad. When I traced his history back I found that, an unregistered Welsh Cob, he had been bred just above Tregaron out of a Welsh Cob mare by a Welsh Cob stallion, and he was supposed to have been castrated as a yearling. He was bought by a young girl, but in actual fact he had been only partly castrated, and was still a rig. The girl loved horses, but tended to treat them as children, and by the time he was three years old she was terrified of Potty. She sold him to someone who attempted unsuccessfully to break him, then Potty was trailed yet again to Llanybyther horse sale – this was the third time he had visited the market – and was bought by an acquaintance of mine who was quite sure that he could sort out this very handsome, but completely unmanageable, three-year-old.

First he tried to beat him into submission. And when this didn't work he starved him. After starving him of food and water for three days, he got on his back and tried to gallop him into submission. Potty got him off and attacked him when he was on the ground so he was sold again and sent to me to break.

When he arrived he was so round the bend that anyone going into the stable did so at considerable risk. He would either attack them with his front feet, and teeth, or kick them. And he had his own particular brand of trick: if he could get someone into a corner, he would back up against them and proceed to push and push.

The first thing I did was to put Strawberry, my daughter Paddy's pony, into the loose box with him for a couple of days. I went in every now and then to feed and talk to him quietly, until he began to lose a little bit of fear, and be slightly less hostile.

Then on the third day I had an early breakfast to give myself plenty of time to get Potty sorted out in the stable. The first thing I had to do of course was to put a halter on him. This was impossible by normal methods, since as soon as he saw the halter, he'd attack you. So when I went in with the halter, I was careful to keep Strawberry between myself and Potty all the time, and eventually after about an hour and a half, using Strawberry as a shield, I managed to get a halter on to him. Then I tied him up short to the partition, and still using Strawberry as a shield I got him saddled and bridled. Then I got on to him. He bucked solidly for ten minutes, but it was a comparatively easy buck to sit, and having found that this tactic had failed, he proceeded to bolt. I didn't make the mistake that most people make on a bolting horse: I didn't try to stop him, all I did was to give him slack rein and let him gallop. The only time I touched the rein was to prevent him from galloping straight into something, when I leant over and pulled him away from the object he was galloping towards. After a further ten minutes Potty had had enough, so he went quite quietly for the rest of that day.

The following day, after bucking for a couple of minutes, he went off again for two or three hundred yards, then realizing the futility of it he settled down for the next twenty minutes or so, only to go suddenly up on his hind legs, trying to come over backwards. This is a very nasty little trick, but it's quite easy to cure. All you do is slip off over his tail, and when the horse comes down again vault back into the saddle over his backside. This sounds very difficult, but in actual fact it's purely a question of timing. Again finding himself frustrated, Potty went quite happily that day.

Over the next three weeks he tried every trick I'd ever seen in a bad horse, other than laying down and rolling on top of me. But at the end of three months he was going quite nicely and quietly for me, though he wasn't yet a very safe conveyance for anyone else. Eventually he was extremely lucky in his purchaser, who, whilst being extremely firm, was also sympathetic, so Potty gradually regained his sanity and became an extremely good Welsh Cob.

Just as malnutrition and ill-treatment can break a horse both mentally and physically, so can boring, monotonous work. A good example of such lethargy is the trekking pony which does nothing but walk day after day with complete beginners on his back, at the rate of about two miles per hour. A lively, active pony can change into a bored, sulky individual in a single trekking season, and even two or three months of nothing but trekking can completely ruin a pony.

So it can be seen that handling, nutrition, breeding and the type of work that a horse has been doing are all factors that have to be taken into account when you are assessing the psychological make-up of a horse.

We know from our own experience of course that the intelligence of horses varies considerably, but no work has been done on the inheritance of intelligence in horses. Two gentlemen called Williams and Thompson however, did a considerable amount of work on intelligence in rats, in 1954. They selected the most intelligent rats and the least intelligent rats of a group, and for six generations they interbred the most intelligent rats, and the least intelligent ones. They discovered that breeding from the most intelligent rats they could increase their intelligence three-fold. Among the least intelligent rats intelligence had decreased in the same ratio. Their work was of considerable assistance to us, since their description of how they assessed intelligence in rats gave us pointers as to just how we could gauge the intelligence of our horses.

Since it has been shown that intelligence in rats is inherited, and that intelligence in human beings is also inherited, it is probable that the intelligence in horses too is inherited. And if intelligence is inherited, excitability, laziness and other personality factors, we thought, may be inherited too. A foal from a dominant mare, therefore, is himself likely to be dominant, not only from example, but also partly because of his heredity. This factor is something that has been neglected by the commercial breeder, since a sober, stable disposition isn't usually a marketable factor. Indeed in some cases, bad tempered and bloodyminded mares have been put to extremely excitable and unmanageable stallions, simply because the stallion is the right colour, and has the right show points. Yet excitability, emotionality and savageness have all proved to be hereditary in rats, so it is likely that they are hereditary factors in horses.

We also know that environment has been proved scientifically to have a considerable effect on intelligence in human beings: difference in environment can affect human beings' intelligence by as much as twenty-two percent. This too tends to confirm scientifically what every horseman has known for a long time: that temperament can be affected both by heredity *and* training.

What we wanted to know now was more exactly how horse personality was formed, and what we could do to influence our own horses.

4: *Motivations of Horse Behaviour – And How To Use Them*

What makes a horse tick? What makes a horse do this rather than that? This is a fascinating question because what motivates a horse lies behind everything that it does, and when you can discover what makes a horse do something, you can apply it to your advantage, and improving the performance of your horse will give you satisfaction beyond words. But finding what motivates a horse is always frustrating, because it is like looking for a needle under a blanket: you are probing around in the dark, and you only know you have found it when it sticks into you, and makes you jump. You can never *see* the reason why the horse does something because that is hidden away somewhere in his head. You can only see the result of the reason. The best you can do is to guess what motive lies behind what he is doing, and test out your theory afterwards. That has been our work over the last twenty years.

We made one of our successful guesses with Bella. Bella came to us as an untouched four-year-old, but within six or eight weeks of being gentled, she started shying very badly. Now we worked out that she could be shying for any of five reasons. She could be shying out of boredom or fear; from habit; from a sense of insecurity, and lack of confidence; or out of sheer bloody-mindedness, trying it on with her rider; or from any combination of these things.

From observing her in the field we noticed that when she was being driven with the other horses, she hardly shied at anything, so we knew it wasn't habit, or any very serious fear. We also knew it wasn't boredom because we were trying to keep her work as varied and interesting as possible. But she was being ridden by a girl who was rather a weak rider. So we concluded

59

it might be slight fear of strange objects, but that mainly it was a combination of lack of confidence in herself, and in her rider. She was a dominant member of her group, so we concluded also that she might be trying it on with a weak rider.

The cure was comparatively simple. First, I rode her myself for a week; then I made sure that she continued to be ridden by a strong rider, so that she not only gained increased confidence in her rider and herself, but also had no chance of trying it on. Second, since there was the possibility that fear was involved, I made quite sure by gazing at any strange object that we came across myself, and drawing her attention to it, that she saw it properly. And after a week or two she went back to riding in her normal quiet and sweet way.

All our work in horse psychology has in fact been aimed at making accessible to the ordinary horseman the skill that comes to the great horse handlers instinctively. They already know, by intuition, what makes a horse do certain things, and it is for this reason that they are top class horsemen. We who are not quite so gifted need to acquire our knowledge more laboriously. We have to deduce the motive from the action of the horse. If, for example, we know that the horse has not been fed for forty-eight hours, and he asks for food, we deduce that he is asking because he is hungry. If on the other hand the horse has been fed within the last half hour, and is still screaming for food, we know that he is just plain greedy. But of course behaviour is not always as easy to interpret as this, and a wrong deduction may simply compound the problem.

If, for instance, your horse, like Bella, is shying, you may have been able to reduce the possible reasons to two: either he is bored, and looking for something to make his life a bit more exciting; or he tends to be a bit sleepy and doesn't notice the object, so it startles him. If the reason is the first, and he is bored, then he needs to be punished to stop him shying. But if on the other hand he was fast asleep, and the object startled him, and you punish him, he will then associate pain with the object he shied at: if it is a white paper bag that startles him, and you punish him, he will then associate white paper bags with pain, and instead of curing him you will simply have made him shy at white paper bags.

Motivation is an all-inclusive term covering just about anything that makes a horse act, or respond. The term comes from the Latin word meaning to move, and if we think of motivation as the mover of the horse, the cause of the horse moving, we won't be very far wrong. But it is convenient to the study of horse behaviour to divide motivations into two separate categories: physical and emotional.

The drives to satisfy physical needs – the requirements of the body – are inborn in all horses, to a greater or lesser degree. When a horse is hungry he is driven by hunger to find food; when he is thirsty, his thirst drives him to find water; and when a mare is in season her body drives her to find a stallion. Mother Nature takes great care of her children, especially her favourite child, the horse, so she provides him with the instinct to know exactly what he needs and how to get it. If a horse is short of one particular sort of food, Nature will drive him to look for exactly that food. This instinct of course goes back to the primitive horse who ranged over enormous areas searching for various different grasses to balance his diet. For Nature has taught the horse to be a selective feeder, unlike the cow who eats everything available.

I watched this careful selectivity in a group of 'wild' horses not long ago. When we have to catch a pony out of a bunch that runs free in the mountain, I like to observe the herd for two or three days to observe their habits: where they spend the night, which line of grazing they take, where they drink, and where they shelter in bad weather. This is a labour-saving device, to enable me to pick the easiest place to drive them off the mountain to a spot where I can catch the horse I select. And since I had this time to catch two ponies out of a particular herd, I had an excuse to spend two glorious June days sitting in an assortment of sunny spots observing the ponies grazing. The only drawback was having to get up early. But the inconvenience of leaving home before dawn in June is more than compensated for by what you see when you get out on the mountain.

I knew from previous observations where the ponies had spent the night, and I was in position just before dawn. As the sun rose over the other side of the valley I could see the ponies sleeping below me. There were five or six mares and foals, half a dozen yearlings and two-year-olds, and the two three-year-olds that I wanted to catch, all sleeping in a tight group within an area of about fifty yards. Most of the mares were standing with their heads drooping over their foals, who were lying stretched out under their noses. And round the main body of the mares were a group of last year's foals, and the two-year-olds, also fast asleep. As the sun began to warm them, first one foal then another raised its head, saw it was time to get up, scrambled shakily to its feet and shook itself. Then each one stretched, first its head and neck, then its back and finally its hind legs, one at a time. Feeling hungry, without exception, they all then went and had breakfast at the milk bar. Having done this they proceeded to play, disturbing the yearlings and two-year-olds, who were sleeping a bit late.

The newly awakened herd proceeded to take the knife-edge off their appetite by cropping the short sweet grass near their sleeping place. But slowly, one by one, led by an old white mare who had long ceased to bear foals but who was still the leader of the herd, they ambled off, picking a mouthful here and there, down to the stream for a drink. The old mare drank first, as the others drifted in ones and twos down to the water. No sooner had she slaked her thirst than she climbed up the other side of the stream to a vantage point where she could observe danger, whilst the rest of the herd drank. When they had finished drinking they made their way up the hill to the mare, and she in turn set off to higher ground where the grass was more abundant. The others followed her, still picking a mouthful of heather here and there, and eventually, half a mile further on, they came to the spot the old mare had selected for their breakfast. Everyone got his or her head down and started tearing at the young grasses, as if there was never going to be another meal. Then they moved on another mile or so to a south-facing slope of a higher valley.

Here the mares took a nap, whilst the foals indulged in a bit of horse play and tag. Every now and then one of the smaller foals would be getting the worst of it, so it would flee from its bigger companions to hide behind its mother. It would stay there for a minute or two, then peep around her backside to see what the others were doing. And you could see it weighing the pleasure of playing against the chance of getting hurt again. In a state of indecision it would have a quick snack, then slowly edge back towards the playing foals, and by degrees join in the game of tag again. This ritual was repeated over and over again until about half past ten, when the mares decided they were thirsty again. So they made their way slowly down to another stream, again preceded by the old mare, who after drinking walked up to a vantage point whilst the rest of the herd drank. From here they went to another grazing spot. This time instead of the shorter grass, they were grazing a mixture of heather and coarse grass. From here they moved on to yet another resting spot. They drank and grazed in this way three times more, each time choosing a different type of grass in a completely different place. And each time they drank they chose a different stream. In all during the day they had five different grazing periods, five different sleeping periods, and the foals had five different playing periods, with journeys varying from half a mile to a mile between each. The circle eventually completed was over three miles between its two widest points. What struck me was how after each resting period the old grey mare knew exactly where she was going, she knew what type of grass they needed next. Whether they drank from five different streams because the water in each too provided something different, I don't know.

Just before the sun started setting the ponies were back in their sleeping place. And it was here I decided that I would catch the two I was after, because there was a convenient lane down to a farm nearby.

I thought a lot that day about how deliberate was the feeding pattern I was observing: how when the horses were eating the coarse grass and heather, they tended to take off the tips only; how, apart from picking odd bits here and there between grazing spots, the herd grazed where the old mare told them, and yet how carefully she had chosen a variety of foods.

We knew from our own experience that all horses don't necessarily have the same nutritional needs. In fact my wife and I once had an argument as to whether or not our horses were getting enough salt. So I conducted a series of trials.

First of all I mixed one ounce of salt with ten ounces of earth and gave each horse a fragment of the resulting paste with his feed. All of the twenty or so horses we had in at that time thought this a joke in very poor taste, with the sole exception of Grayling, who licked up all the mixture of earth and salt. So I knew Grayling needed salt very badly. The following day, I mixed four ounces of salt with twelve ounces of soil, and that day two more horses licked the mixture of earth and salt. I moved on from one quarter salt in the earth, to a half, to three-quarters, and when I finally got to pure salt only Biddy and Spitfire left it. This was one argument I lost: we proved that of the twenty horses, one had a desperate need for salt, and only two didn't need salt at all. So I adjusted the salt in their feed accordingly.

Through a very simple trial such as this one, it is possible to determine the bodily needs of any particular horse. And since each horse is completely different from the next, it is very important to establish early on what your horse needs for his bodily wellbeing. The need for liquid, for instance, can be measured very simply. All you have to do is to measure the amount of water you offer him each day, and work out the average he drinks over a period of at least five days. This test of course must also be related to weather conditions, and the amount of work he is doing.

Over a period of years with a large number of horses, we have found one horse who needed as little as three gallons of water per day and another who drank eighteen gallons a day. Of these, the one drinking only three gallons of water was in the stable during a very clammy, damp period, whilst the eighteen gallons a day was drunk by a horse doing moderate work during very hot dry weather.

It is easy enough to assume, if your horse seems in general good health and happy, that you have given him all the food and water he needs. Most of us do that. But it is only by observing *exactly* how much he needs of hay, corn, water, salt and minerals, that you can get to know your horse really intimately. The results of the conscious study of the horse's basic needs in themselves may indeed be superfluous; but by making this conscious study you will be subconsciously studying him as well, and you will absorb a great deal of unconscious knowledge of his mental needs.

Rostellan is a typical case in point. His bodily need to keep him in good condition for hunting and minor competition work, is twelve to fourteen pounds of corn a day, but he is quite capable, if he gets the chance, of eating twenty-one pounds of corn a day. Once he got as fat as a pig, and was jumping out of his skin on this diet but because of the increased body weight he was putting much greater strain than usual on both his heart and his legs. So to know the upper limit of his food consumption was as important as it was to know how much he needed to keep him in good health. It helped us to measure his greed factor – Rostellan had a greed factor of fifty percent, that is he would eat fifty percent more food than he actually needed for his bodily condition, and this helped us to know Rostellan better.

Here, mixed up with bodily requirements, was a more complex need, determined by the inner life of the horse. Such needs are the need for love, the approval of his owner, and the respect of the other members of the herd. None of these needs is purely physical, but it is compelling all the same. The horse has a need for varied outlook, he needs a change from everyday things, he also needs bodily movement and a certain amount of light for his mental well-being. These are the needs we have taken great trouble to identify, because although you can force a horse to do so much with brute force and ignorance, he will do far more if he is satisfying a drive within himself.

Some of these internal needs are like smoking cigarettes: they are addictive, so the more you give him, the more he needs. When you first get a young untouched horse, for instance, he doesn't know what praise and approval are, and since he has never had them, he doesn't need them. But the more praise and approval you give a young horse, the more he will do to get more praise and approval, and constantly excel himself to get the praise he needs. In fact I use praise with my horses constantly, and of course disapproval, for mere disapproval from the owner can be a very severe punishment in itself.

At Penrice one-day event, in the spring, I used this technique on Biddy. She was horseing, and she went extremely badly, so after we had finished I didn't touch her with a stick, but I voiced my displeasure, and when I got off her I completely ignored her. Someone else groomed her, put her away, fed and watered her. I didn't go near her for five days. If I passed her box I ignored her completely – of course, someone else fed, groomed, watered and exercised her for me, under strict instruction not to praise her in any way whatever. At the end of five days, when I got on her, she was turning herself inside out to please. I took her up to our one-day event course and put her over all the stiffest fences in the most difficult possible way. They were far worse than anything that she had had to face five days previously, but she jumped them all superbly. And then of course she got her praise. My disapproval had been the most severe punishment that I could give her. So the following one-day event, even though it was only her second, she finished eleventh, having the fastest cross-country time of the day.

Rostellan on the other hand is a great deal more difficult to deal with. He is like a naughty small boy, always getting up to one sort of mischief or another. Among the tricks he has taught himself is to unbolt his stable door and let himself out. We usually have a series of barricades and bolts that he can't reach to stop him doing this. But occasionally the bars and bolts are not put properly in their place, which is what happened one morning, just after he had been groomed. There he was beautifully clean, with his mane and tail brushed out ready to take part in a showjumping competition at the Riding Club, when we left him to get changed ourselves. When I came out the first thing I saw was that Rostellan's door was open. The next thing I saw was that he had opened the front gate. And just inside the front gate was a dirty great patch of mud.

Fortunately my wife had not seen him yet, so I shouted, 'Rostellan', and he came bolting and bucking down the road, trotted up to his stable and put himself back in, knowing he had been extremely naughty. When he heard my wife coming out through the front door, he retreated cowering to the corner of his box, peering round the corner of the door to see what sort of a temper she was going to be in. When she saw the mud over his freshly brushed coat and she heard what he had done, she started to scold him. But it was no good. She couldn't go through with it. The sight of a very dirty Rostellan cowering and trying to disappear through the back wall of his loose box was too much for her, and she simply had to laugh. You can't be disapproving when you are laughing.

Rostellan immediately swaggered to the front of the box to tell everyone how clever he was, and I decided to disappear and get a bucket of hot water to wash the worst of the mud off. My wife did her best to repair the damage to his mane and tail.

A horse may also be stimulated by something outside himself, rather than by an inner drive. I was able to observe a whole series of actions and reactions in response to external stimuli when I spent an hour recently watching Spitfire's foal Spit Again, commonly known as Gain. It was early on a fine May morning, and Spitfire and Gain were fast asleep in a sunny corner of the field, Gain stretched out in his favourite posture under Spitfire's nose. He was completely relaxed, soaking up the warmth of the sun and the security generated by the presence of his mother. When he heard me coming into the field, he raised his head, looked up and then, very slowly, got to his feet. When he was more or less vertical, he started stretching: first one leg, then another, then his back, and finally he stretched his neck. He stood watching me for a minute or two, then something moved in the hedge behind him. He jumped forward startled, and then trotted twenty or thirty yards away from the noise, to which his first reaction was one of fear. When he had reached a safe distance, however, he turned to see what had startled him. It was a half-grown fox who had come out of the hedge and was trotting down it.

This stimulated his curiosity, so he trotted towards the cub to investigate. The cub quickened his pace to a canter, Gain reacted with excitement, and gave chase. But the fox cub dodged back into the hedge. Unable to follow him, Gain slid to a halt.

The hedge, in stopping him, could be called in the context a negative stimulus: for something that makes a horse do something need not necessarily be positive, it can be negative, in that it stops him doing something else, in this case moving.

He then saw a particularly succulent patch of grass, which, after the exercise he had just taken, put an edge on his hunger, so he went over and grazed for the next twenty minutes. When his hunger was satisfied he stopped grazing – again the satisfaction of his hunger being a negative stimulus to stop him grazing – and decided he was tired again so he slept standing up in the sun until about ten minutes later the sun clouded over and a shower of rain began beating into his face. This was uncomfortable, so he turned round to point his back to the rain. The shower had passed over and about five minutes later a group of trekking ponies went past the end of the field. Again his interest was aroused, so he cantered across the field, stopping only when he ran into a barbed wire fence by the road. The wire hurt, making him shy away.

From this account of a single hour in a foal's life, external stimuli provoked fear, curiosity, hunger, sleep: made him move away, move towards and stop. Indeed, each stimulus could be seen either as creating movement or stopping movement. Some of the movements were violent and some very minute, such as the movement of the jaws as he was eating. But all had been externally provoked.

It is providing such external stimuli – the right stimuli to provoke the reaction you require – that is important when you are riding a horse. Horsemen tend to think that the only way to teach a horse is by repetitive training, using a bit and heels to stop him or to stimulate him. This of course as far as it goes is fine. But if you can extend the number of stimuli you use to make a horse *want* to do something, it is possible to extend the performance of the horse itself.

If you analyse the stimulus-reaction sequence in horse behaviour you will see that if the stimulus comes first, the second phase is a desire to do something. The stimulus, whether from inside the horse or from outside it, awakens a desire; and the desire in turn drives it to *do* something to satisfy it. So if a horse is thirsty (internal physical stimulus), this will awaken a desire for water, and he will walk until he finds water. Then he will drink to satisfy his thirst. So his thirst has made him do two things, walk and then drink, the first being designed to achieve the second.

Hunger and thirst and avoiding pain are all bodily needs which can be satisfied. But the need for excitement is an emotional need, within the horse's mind, which also demands satisfaction. The need for excitement to alleviate boredom is perfectly illustrated in Bluebell, a three-year-old black cross Welsh Cob gelding, thirteen-three hands high, whom we had on our farm for a while. He was in need of constant excitement, and when he was feeling bored he used to go and tease Madam. Madam was the herd boss – mainly because she was extremely bad tempered and clobbered anything that came near her. Bluebell would try to get the other young horses to play, but if they wouldn't he would wander over to where Madam was sleeping or grazing. She would put her ears back and raise one hind leg, and he would retreat a pace or two. Then he would take a step forward, and stick his head out. Madam would swing round and try to have a piece out of him. He would turn towards her again. And saunter up again with his head out. This time she would probably flick out with one hoof. Bluebell would dodge the kick quickly, and again edge round her. He'd keep this up for ten or fifteen minutes until Madam had finally had enough, and chased him half around the field – which is what he wanted in the first place, since he knew he had the legs of Madam.

At one time Cork Beg was friendly with a bull. We had no other horse at the time, so he was turned out with the bull and they grazed together and slept together, the bull lying down and old Cork Beg resting a leg, with his head nodding over the bull. But the old man couldn't stand still for very long and eventually he would saunter away and start grazing. Then to alleviate his boredom he would come dancing up to the bull and pretend to box him. The bull would put his head down and roar at Cork Beg and the old man would continue to tease the bull until the bull charged him. Cork Beg would swing to one side as the bull charged, the bull would go lumbering past, and Cork Beg would turn in pursuit, trying to bite at the root of the bull's tail. The bull would stop and charge again, Cork Beg would flee this time, and this game would go on for ten minutes to a quarter of an hour, until the old man had got his excitement and the bull had had enough. Whereupon the bull would really charge Cork Beg seriously and Cork Beg would kick at his face and take the best possible means of escape.

Both these examples show how, if a horse is bored, he will actively court danger to get a bit of excitement. Excitement in other words is a very real need that must be satisfied.

Hunger for food, thirst for water, the need for excitement and the need to escape from boredom, thus all provide a horse with reasons for doing something. And the third phase in the cycle is the achievement of the object: when the thirsty horse finds water, drinks and satisfies the thirst, ending the motivational cycle for the time being.

There are, then, three distinct phases in any motivational cycle. The first stage is the stimulus that initiates the movement – the stimulus of thirst, which makes the horse move. The second stage is the movement itself – walking toward the water. The third phase is the achievement of the initial object, in this case having a drink of water.

This cycle of motivation plays an integral part in success in competition and I made full use of it with Biddy in the cross-country at a recent Welsh one-day event, held at Builth Wells. Biddy, whose name is officially Esther Aeron, is an extremely good horse for a cross-country course, but unfortunately like all women she tends to be a little bit temperamental. Biddy needs love and approval. She is also very proud, and like any thorough-bred needs to expend energy, so she wants a lot of excitement – all these things are characteristic of any good competition horse. Further, the energy Biddy expends is both nervous and physical so to excel in competition she has to be extremely fit both mentally and physically. You go to a lot of trouble to build up this energy within the horse, which then needs release. And since Biddy loves jumping, she expends her pent-up nervous and physical energy by jumping and galloping.

Just before we start competitions of this sort, Biddy is usually dancing round all over the place, and it is extremely difficult to get her to stand stationary for the starter. On this occasion, just before we were due to start, I got her to walk the last two or three strides, to halt for two seconds and when the starter's hand came down we were away.

The first fence was bales with a pole on top. She tore into this, and flew it. We then had a very sharp corner with a big combination fence of two three-foot-six telegraph poles. And then two strides, and a four-foot parallel standing at the maximum three-foot-six. I steadied her with my hands and voice, 'Steady girl. Steady girl. Slowly. Slowly, gently,' and brought her well back on to her hocks. The last second was just an explosion of energy which flew her over the first section, she bounced for one stride, and I drove my heels into her just to give her extra incentive over the parallel of two poles. The next fence was a pile of tree trunks, three foot high and seven foot at the base. By now she was well into her stride, and really galloping, and I didn't need to do anything. I just sat still, and at the last second gave her her head. And she flew them like a steeple chaser.

It was about three hundred yards to the next fence and we were really going: in fact we were going so fast that I had a job steadying her. We had to go up on to a bank and jump over a low V-fence with a five-foot drop on the other side. When I finally steadied her, she dropped back to a walk and just popped over without any difficulty whatsoever. We flew over the paling fence which came next, and then we came to one of the most difficult fences on the course: a three-foot wall, one bounce stride, and then a post and rail. 'Steady girl, slowly girl, steady girl.' I managed to get her back by using only my voice. She popped on to the bank and bounced out over the rails. Almost before I was back in the saddle she was belting on at the next fence as fast as she could go. This was a gate, which she rocketed over.

We were really motoring now. Fences eight, nine and ten she took in her stride. We had to go down a steep bank to fence number eleven, which was a set of steps. As we got to the top of the bank, she skidded to a halt, went down the other side, almost sliding on her bottom, then popped over the steps. The bull pen had to be taken at an angle, one step over, one step out, and away again over the next three fences.

Biddy was really enjoying herself. In fact it was hard to decide who was enjoying it most, Biddy or myself. The speed at which she was going into the fences was incredible: great long raking strides, and taking each fence as if it were her last meal. The water trough, the log piles, the pedestrian crossing, and the ski jump all floated away beneath us. The sheep pen provided some difficulty, because Biddy was going much too fast at it and I was having a job to steady her, but she flew over the corner, and over the next brush fence too. Then we came to the coffin fence, which was a solid fence with a drop to the water, over the water and up out over a post and rails. She did this with spectacular grace and ease, and flew into the last fence as if it was the first. And we were home with nearly a minute to spare.

As that story shows, I had made use of the horse's own need to expend energy, and satisfied her need for excitement and praise, and her pride. By using my reins and heels I had used additional external stimuli to steady her and to drive her over fences. Fortunately since she is a very good free-going horse, I hadn't had to use my stick at all. But I would have used the stick, and provided the stimulus of pain to make her jump a fence, if she had been reluctant to do so. But the important ingredient of success was the fact that that underlying need Biddy has to excel and receive praise and admiration, had been satisfied.

From this it can be seen how just by harnessing the various motivational drives within the horse it is possible with a competitive horse to achieve outstanding cross-country performances.

Some of these motivational drives are positive, and where possible these are the ones we stress in dealing with horses. Others are negative – pain, for example. Or if you watch a foal you will see a whole variety of negative drives in action. A foal sees something, is frightened by it, and will run away and hide behind its mother. The drive this time is fear; but when he gets to his mother the fear will subside.

In comparing examples of positive and negative drives we note that they play completely different roles. A positive stimulus arises directly from a motive: a horse is thirsty, he searches for water, and he finds water and quenches his thirst. In the case of a negative stimulus, the stimulus *causes* the drive: the foal is frightened by something, and it runs away to escape, and to gain the protection of its mother. The easiest way to think of it is thus: the horse moves towards a positive goal, and away from a negative goal. If you think of a small boy reaching for a packet of sweets, and escaping from a kick on the backside, the sweets are the positive goal, and the kick on the backside, which is painful, is the negative goal.

Robert Louis Stevenson during his *Travels with a Donkey* got the donkey going with two sticks. On the end of one long stick, he dangled a carrot and at the end of another he had a pin. And he used to dangle the carrot in front of the donkey's nose while at the same time applying the pin to his rump. So the donkey naturally wanted to go towards the carrot and away from the pain of the pin. Here you have positive and negative stimulus used simultaneously.

It is far *easier* to set about training an animal, especially a horse, using pain and fear. The memory of pain and fear will stay with the horse far longer than the memory of a pleasant experience, and it is extremely difficult to eradicate. And the horse, after an unpleasant experience, will associate similar situations with the pain and the fear a long time afterwards. But it is not necessarily the most effective.

Jezebel illustrates this point perfectly. We got Jezebel because no one could catch her, or do anything with her. Her fear of a confined space was such that she would jump a six-foot wall, half jumping and half climbing, rather than stay in a yard. She had run wild on the Preseli Mountains as a yearling and a two-year-old, and she had been born with two things: a temper with a very low boiling point, and a fantastic jumping ability. So when her owners wanted to catch her, and she was driven into a yard for the first time, when she had never been handled in her life, her fear of man made her take the easiest way of escape, jumping out over the gate. But they needed to catch her, so she was driven back into the yard again, with some difficulty. Everyone's tempers got a bit frayed in the process, so they stationed people round the yard with sticks to make sure she didn't try and jump out again.

She took the very simple expedient of charging, and jumping out over the lowest point and the smallest man. She then got herself hit over the head, which increased her fear. This process was compounded again and again, each time they tried to catch her, so by the time we got her she was not only terrified of all human beings, but she hated them as well. Overcoming this fear and hatred was a major problem which took me a very long time to solve.

She now has her own stable, and all we need to do to get her in is to drive her down the road, and she trots straight in and stands there. Occasionally when she is feeling a bit bored she'll decide to cut up rough with the old man, but there is no real fear or enthusiasm in it. She merely does it to annoy me. It has taken me three or four hundred attempts and endless patience and understanding to achieve this – sometimes it took us three or four hours to get her in without frightening or upsetting her – all to overcome at most a dozen unpleasant early experiences.

This is why when we are gentling a horse, in the early stages we try to avoid any conflict at all, and above all we take pains not to frighten the horse.

A very difficult horse, who tested our capacity to do this to the limit, was called the Bishop, because he belonged to a Dr Dean. He was sent to us as a five-year-old, unbroken and unbreakable. Fortunately we had stipulated that he should have shoes on when he came, and he arrived about four o'clock one afternoon whilst I was milking. As soon as I had finished milking my father and I had tea, and made a start on him. We had a lot of difficulty getting a saddle on because, as soon as we tried to girth him up, he started bucking and kicking. So we took the girth and stirrups and stirrup leathers off the saddle, and for the next forty minutes we just lifted the saddle on and off his back, until instead of exploding each time the saddle came near him he was half asleep, chewing out of his manger, when we put the saddle on his back. When we could leave the saddle there without him firing it off, we attached a single girth to one side and put the saddle on and off again another dozen times. The first time the girth was put across his back, his back came up like a bow ready to fire an arrow, but there was so little difference between having the girth on the saddle and not, that after two or three times he took no further notice of it. Then we left the saddle on with the girth dangling for a couple of minutes. Then my father, being very careful not to touch him with the girth, handed the girth through to me and I buckled it on to the bottom hole. As soon as I had done this, he eased it up his side a hole. Then I eased it up my side a couple of holes, until it was just touching his chest. Immediately he stopped eating. And up came

his back again. We left him a couple of minutes, and when nothing else happened, and down came his back and he started
eating again, we put the second girth on in exactly the same way.
Again when it touched him, up came his back, and again after a
minute or so it came down again. Then I tightened up the first
girth another hole. The Bish exploded. But the saddle was on
firmly enough now for us to leave him to his own devices for a
couple of minutes.

Eventually when the saddle was still in place and no one was
taking any notice of his gyrations, he stopped bucking, went back
to his manger and started eating again. And I tightened the
second girth up a couple of holes. And again the Bish exploded.
Each time he exploded we just left him to his own devices, until
he had had enough of his blowing and bouncing, and in this way
eventually we got the girth tightened and firm, put on the stirrups
and bridle, and took him outside on the end of a long rope. As
soon as he got out of the door he started bucking again, so again
we just left him to buck with the stirrups flapping, standing at
the full length of the rope. He bucked round in a circle for five
minutes or so, with me pivoting as he went, but talking to him
quietly and gently all the time. 'There's a bloody fool, there's a
bloody fool, who's the bloody stupid fellow, who's a bloody stupid
fellow. Who's a bloody fool' – repeating this over and over in a
singsong voice.

Eventually since no one was worrying and no one was excited,
he stopped bucking, and I went over and made a fuss of him.
Then we led him down to the breaking field, which was a two-
acre field, and absolutely dead flat. This was important in the
case of the Bish, since I had a pretty good idea that as soon as
I got on him he was going to start bucking, and the last thing that
I wanted him to do with me was to buck downhill. Every few
strides toward the field the Bish would start bucking again, but
I let him get to the end of the rope, talking to him all the time,
and whenever he had finished bucking, we went on. When at last
we got to the field, my father eased me up so that I was leaning
across the saddle. As expected, as soon as he felt my weight on

his back the Bish exploded again. I just slid off, and allowed him to buck in his circle. He was getting a bit bored with this, and after four or five bucks he had stopped again, so my father eased me on to his back again, again he exploded, and again I slid off. This went on for about a quarter of an hour, until eventually he allowed me to lean across the saddle. I made a terrific fuss of him and he stood still, enjoying being told what a clever horse he was – for once.

Next time, I eased myself so that I was sitting upright on his back, and got my feet into the stirrups. My father undid the long rope, and led him forward. As soon as he had taken a couple of steps, he exploded. But one of the advantages in breaking a big sixteen-three thoroughbred horse is that he will usually buck in a straight line, and sitting a big strong buck in a straight line is rather like sitting on a very superior rocking horse. After three or four circuits of the field, with me showing my enjoyment, Bish decided that it wasn't worth expending all that energy for no purpose. So he slowed down to a canter. I let him canter round the field a couple of times, he slowed to a trot, and eventually I settled him down to a steady walk. Talking, talking, talking all the time. When he stopped I started him again: a couple of strides, then a couple of bucks. But by now the Bish was fairly worn out. So I slid off his back and we led him back to the stable, rubbed him down, gave him a feed and a drink, and left him for the night.

I spent the next day putting the saddle on and off, and riding him for half an hour in the afternoon. This was largely another rodeo performance, but again it ended up with a gentle walk and a trot when he had had enough bucking.

That night I phoned up the Master. I knew the hounds were meeting near Smallwood, which was about two miles away, the next day, but I wanted to find out where the first draw was. My wife and I left next morning aiming to get there just before hounds. I was on the Bishop and my wife was on Cork Beg, who had then been going for a couple of years and was considered reasonably sane. The Bishop proceeded to the Meet in a series of bucks and plunges. We were a bit earlier than we would have liked, because we had to hang about for ten minutes to a quarter of an hour before the hounds found, but we were very lucky, because the fox broke quickly, came out on our side of the cover, and crossed quite near us with hounds hard on his heels. As soon as they had gone a couple of minutes I pointed the Bishop in the direction they had gone, and drove my heels into him. Four or five bucks later we came to the bank at the side of the field. I drove my heels into him again, which stimulated the Bishop into giving an extra large buck and brought him up on top of the bank. Another buck took him off the bank. Cork Beg had jumped in front of us and was cantering across the field. The Bishop followed him in a series of bucks, and when we came in to the second bank, I used the same technique of driving my heels into him so that he bucked on to the bank and off again. But half way across the second field the Bishop was beginning to realize what it was all about, and he was enjoying himself. He stopped bucking and started galloping. When we got to the third bank, because it was the only way he knew to negotiate it, he bucked again, but towards the far side of the fourth field he passed Cork Beg, stood back and rocketed beautifully over the fourth bank.

By now the Bishop was really enjoying himself. The hounds ran for about another mile and a half before driving their fox to ground, and we were in sight of them all the time. After that I thought the Bishop had had enough for the first time, and so we went home.

From that time the Bishop stopped bucking altogether. Or rather, the only time he ever bucked after that was from *joie de vivre*, when he would put in two or three almighty bucks just to show he was really enjoying himself.

It is true that, with time and patience, we might have got him going right using almost any method. We could have broken his spirit completely using tough rough methods. Or we could have spent endless hours long-reining, and working him on the ground before riding him. But by showing him straight away that being ridden was fun, we achieved our object quickly and with the minimum of trouble. We had got a very difficult 'unbreakable' horse enjoying himself and wanting to work, and what is more we had made life easier and more enjoyable for ourselves.

My technique had been to use what I knew of the horse's motivations. For the first part of the hunt I had used his dislike of being ridden, by making him buck in the direction I wanted him to, and by driving my heels into him making him buck even higher, I had negotiated the first two banks. But after that the joy of galloping with other horses, and the desire to be as near hounds as possible, had been all the stimulus that was needed to get him going really well.

The first thing that is involved in training a horse then, is the horse's own innate desires: that is to say, those things that are born in the horse, that he does naturally without any training whatever. The first thing the foal does when it is born is to seek nourishment from his mother. And his mother will push him into her flank to suck. While he is a foal, the milk he drinks gives him both food and liquid, but as he gets older he'll imitate his mother and eat grass and drink water, and if he is in the stable he will eat a little corn as well. So we can see that the need for food and water is born in the foal. Also within the foal is the desire for movement. He will exercise himself, for all horses have to move and keep moving. He will also need a certain amount of excitement. And later on as he gets older his sexual desires will be aroused. The horse also needs air, and needs light. All these things are born in the horse. They are all necessary for his physical and mental wellbeing. If he does not get them he will either die, or become mentally unbalanced.

We can use all these things in training a horse. His desire for food, for example, can be used to tempt him to follow you. His desire for movement and excitement can be used to make him gallop and jump.

But whilst these things are all inborn, they can also be in-

creased or decreased by handling and training. One horse's desire
for movement and excitement may be greater than another's –
we call the horses that have very little desire for movement and
excitement 'lazy' or 'sleepy'. And those that have a very great
desire for movement and excitement we call 'excitable' or 'mad
fellows'. A horse may be a greedy feeder or a shy feeder. Now
these things, whilst they are partly inbred, are also influenced by
the treatment the animal receives. If you starve a horse or if you
overfeed it, his desire for movement lessens; or if you get it very
fit the desire increases. A lot of slow tedious work will make a
horse lazy; a lot of very fast work, galloping and jumping, will
tend to make it hot. All these things must be borne in mind when
you are training a horse. In training a horse what you are basically trying to do is to ingrain habits: when training a horse to
stop on command, you start by saying 'Whoa' as you put pressure
on his mouth. But after a very short time the horse will stop
automatically when you say 'Whoa' whether you touch the reins
or not. This is because he has got into the *habit* of stopping when
you say 'Whoa'!

As I have already said, with a horse you can use one of two
methods of training: you can motivate him by negative goals –
that is you make him do something or perform a certain task to
avoid pain, discomfort or trouble; or you can train a horse by
stimulating his desires, by giving him a positive goal – making
him *want* to do something. You offer him a reward, a titbit or
approval, for doing what you ask. Or you allow him to do something that he does want to do, as a reward for doing something
he does not want to do.

As a simple example of offering a positive goal, when we are
first riding a horse we always ride him with other horses, because he tends to want to follow the other horses, so he goes
quietly and easily, whereas if he were being made to go by himself, he would either tend to stand still, or try to drag us all over
the mountain. If he is following Rostellan, and two or three
others, he regulates his pace to theirs, just because he wants to
stay with his friends.

Most commonly, of course, when you are training a horse, you use a combination of negative and positive goals: you use his desire to avoid pain, and you use his desire for reward. That is, you praise him or make a fuss of him when he does right, and punish him when he does wrong. But once a horse is trained by a negative method, since he is a very intelligent animal, he will do only just enough to avoid punishment and no more. Whereas if you have used praise and rewards, he will expend far greater effort to gain greater praise and greater reward.

It is equally important that when punishment and praise are given, the animal should know what he is being punished or praised for. This is an apparently self-evident fact which in practice is often simply not recognized.

Suppose, for instance, a horse bucks you off. He is immediately rewarded by being able to gallop around free and do what he wants to do. So he is being rewarded for doing something *wrong*. And then if you catch him, and you are feeling angry with him, you give him a clout for bucking you off and galloping away. But as far as the horse is concerned you are hitting him for allowing himself to be caught! This is a very simple example of how a horse can be rewarded for doing wrong, and punished for doing right. Similarly, if a horse jumps an extra large fence, you may punish him by coming half out of the saddle and jagging his mouth as he lands. This sort of thing happens all the time with horses, and makes training extremely difficult.

It is also a very important fact that things learned by *positive* goals are usually forgotten very quickly, so you must constantly be praising and rewarding the animal to reinforce the lesson. Whereas learning by negative goals, that is the avoidance of fear and pain, lasts for a very long time. So if a horse hurts himself, or is punished for doing something that he *should* do, it will be very difficult to eradicate this fear at a later date, in spite of rewarding him when he does the right thing later on. The relevance of this is extremely important. If, for example, a horse is over-fenced jumping and hurts himself, the fear of hurting himself again will remain with him, and tend to be compounded by later experience unless you adopt a very deliberate strategy to see that this does not happen.

For instance, the first time you shoe a horse you may have trouble with him, and find yourself involved in a battle royal. The horse after that will look upon shoeing as an unpleasant experience. And next time you shoe him he will immediately start getting frightened and angry, for, like a human being, when a horse gets frightened he tends to get angry as well. So the second time you have an even greater battle. And this goes on and on until the horse becomes more or less impossible to shoe. It is thus extremely important that the first time you shoe a horse it should be easy; you must never have a battle shoeing if you can possibly help it.

This factor is particularly relevant of course when you are jumping, because if you once make a mistake, and the horse hurts himself, the next time he takes a fence, he will be iffing and butting as he goes into it, so be likely to take off wrongly, which means that he will hurt himself again. And before long you will have a horse that has gone completely off jumping. This happened to me this summer with Biddy. Since Biddy had been schooled specifically for cross-country, her showjumping has always been a bit chancy, and when doing the showjumping section in an event she usually has one or two fences down.

I rode Biddy at Dauncey Park one-day event, in the open section. She adores jumping though she tries to treat the show jumps as steeplechase fences. The showjumping ring at Dauncey was rather small, very tight and twisty, and the jumps were close together. But we went off in great style, and I steadied her nicely over the first two. But we were really motoring by the time we got to the third fence, which meant that she was completely wrong at the fourth, which was a big double of upright rails, the second part of which was a four-foot spread. She went straight into the first part, but was completely wrong at it and when she came to the second part she put in an almighty effort, and caught both rails with her hocks. Somehow we completed the course, but it was a disastrous round. Then we went on to the cross-country, and put in an outstanding performance.

I made the mistake after that of not schooling her over show jumps, but letting her go on doing her cross-country which she adores, and hoping that she would forget about hurting herself showjumping. The next event we took part in was the two-day event at Osberton, and she jumped the first fence with difficulty. Then she refused to jump any more, and it took me nearly two months' careful and quiet schooling to get her showjumping again. This is a simple example of how one careless fence, and one mistake on my part, could completely undo the good work of two years. Even now she is still a little doubtful about her show jumping, though since hurting herself she has probably jumped the best part of a hundred fences successfully. And yet she remembers the one fence at which she hurt herself.

This is a clear example of how a single negative stimulus may be remembered when a hundred positive stimuli may be forgotten.

By just such a process a two- or a three-year-old that gets carved up towards the end of a tough race may never race again, or at the very best will take a very long time before he is really trying once more.

A friend of mine had a very good race horse who had a very slight breathing defect. This had not mattered for two seasons, but by the third, though my friend did not know it, the defect had got worse. The first race that season he managed to win, but because of his restricted breathing, he collapsed between the winning post and the paddock. After about twenty minutes he got up again, and appeared to be all right. But the vet, on examining him, decided that his breathing had gone, and the horse was hobdayed. The following season – twelve months later – he was fit to race again. But after the second fence he just packed it in. He refused to race, and he hasn't run a race since.

This story again illustrates how one unpleasant experience can completely destroy a horse's desire to do something that it has previously done extremely well, and enjoyed doing.

You cannot win a race unless you have the wholehearted enthusiasm and cooperation of the horse. And you can't win a
jumping competition unless the horse is extending every nerve
and fibre to compete and win. So if a horse that has previously
raced and jumped with enthusiasm suddenly takes against racing
or jumping, the best thing you can do is to take it away from
jumping and racing altogether for a time, and do something else
with it, and hope that eventually you can reintroduce it, with
patience and training, to its former skill.

We very often buy race horses that have taken against racing,
and give them a season's hunting before racing them again. And
if one of our own horses suddenly takes against a particular
activity, though we make him complete the task at the time, we
take him away from it completely afterwards. If one of the event
horses suddenly takes against jumping, we put him hacking or
shepherding, then bring him back to jumping very slowly: just
pop him over a few ditches or low fences to start with. Then we
give him a day's hunting, where even if he doesn't jump a fence
all day he will be enjoying himself. This is the important thing
with all horses: they must enjoy themselves in what they are
doing, to do it satisfactorily. The desire to keep with the other
horses out hunting gets them galloping and jumping with enthusiasm, so with time and patience, they will again enjoy galloping and jumping by themselves. With competition jumping one
of the important things is that negotiating a fence must become
a reward in itself. Some horses in fact will only jump out hunting.
They won't jump at home, and they won't jump in competition.

The power of the learned negative goal, so familiar to horsemen, was demonstrated some thirty years ago by an experiment
involving rats (Miller 1948).

A number of white rats were placed one at a time in a white
box separated by a door from a black box. In the floor of the white
compartment was a grid through which a mild electric shock could
be applied. The rats were given a mild shock every five seconds.
Then the door of the box was opened and the shock was turned
on steadily. The rats escaped by running into the adjacent black

box. The sequence was repeated on ten different occasions after which the rats registered terror as soon as they were put inside the white box, even though a shock was not applied. On the five subsequent occasions that the rats were placed in a white box with the door open, the learned fear was strong enough to make them run straight into the black box; and when the door was closed they would force the door open to get out of the box, even though no shock was applied.

This experiment illustrates how pairing the shock with the white wall of the box could cause the colour white to frighten the rats enough to make them force the door. This parallels Biddy's behaviour, when she learned to be afraid not of jumping and jumps – for she continued to jump cross-country fences with enthusiasm – but coloured jumps, because it was on a coloured jump that she had hurt herself. So she associated the colour with pain. She remained quite happy jumping four-foot-six timber. She was refusing to jump two-foot and two-foot-six coloured post and rails.

Most things that a horse fears it didn't fear as a foal. It learned its fears at a later date from its experience, often from experience with man.

5: *Reward and Punishment – Positive and Negative Goals in Training*

Though the whole question of reward and punishment is much more complex than it at first appears to be, at its simplest it is merely a question of giving a horse a handful of nuts when he does the right thing, and clouting him when he does wrong. But what is reward for one animal can be punishment for another.

For example, when Rostellan has done a piece of schooling work particularly well, he is allowed to jump some fences. This is a reward for him, because he loves jumping, and really enjoys competition and performance. On the other hand, Pudding jumps extremely well, but he doesn't enjoy it, and for him to be made to jump is a chore. So what is a reward for Rostellan, is punishment for Pudding.

But the natural inclination of a horse can also be altered by the way it is handled. For animals, like people, are conditioned by their experience. An American researcher demonstrated this very dramatically with some puppies. He wired up pieces of raw meat to an electric current, then showed it to the puppies. They went for the meat, and got an electric shock. He fed the puppies on dried toasted food, and every time they went near the meat he gave them an electric shock. He then took the experiment one stage further by dropping a piece of meat into their boxes, and as he did so turning on the electric current. He eventually brought the poor puppies to such a state of terror that as soon as they saw a piece of meat they started screaming in fear.

It is clear then that the way you present your work to the horse can be very important. When we first started dressage with Biddy for instance, she hated it. She found it boring and monotonous, and her whole attitude showed this. So she did an extremely bad dressage test. We decided to present the work to her in a totally different way, and were able completely to alter her attitude.

I had up to then been doing my dressage with her before taking her out exercising, which meant that the dressage was a prelude to dull and boring work. So I changed the order by doing the dressage work *after* she had exercised, and before she was put back into her stable and fed. This in itself completely changed her attitude, because instead of being a preliminary to the dull monotony of exercising, dressage became the prelude to going in to enjoy her dinner. Her attitude changed visibly. Towards the end of her exercise, before entering the dressage arena, she would start brightening and tightening herself up, and become fully alert. She knew that her dull exercise was over, and she had only another five or ten minutes' work before her meal.

My wife does it differently with Rostellan. She does her dressage work before schooling him in jumping. Again, he knows that the dressage is a prelude to enjoying himself jumping.

Thus a simple change in the timing of your work can change your horse's whole attitude to it. What previously was a dull and boring task becomes a rewarding one for the horse, and with Biddy I have actually achieved the stage where she sees the dressage schooling as the reward for having done her exercise. A full hundred yards from the dressage arena she will draw herself together, arch her back, and bring her head up in preparation for the dressage schooling. So whereas originally the dressage was rewarded with dinner, now it has become itself the reward for exercise.

It is quite possible, in short, to make a horse look on something he has previously looked upon as hard work, or as an unpleasant task, or as punishment, as in fact a *reward*.

Another success of this kind was with a horse called Clear Reason. Clear Reason was a sixteen-two dark brown gelding by High Treason. He had been purchased for a big price as a two-year-old, and put into training. He won one race, and in the following race, when he was odds on favourite, he had had an extremely hard race and got a hiding for his pains. He was beaten into second place and after this he wouldn't race again. They kept him in training the rest of his two-year-old career, and as a three-year-old, hoping he would improve. But he just refused to race.

We bought him as a four-year-old, at a very big price for us in those days. But he was a fine horse with a lot of potential. We schooled him jumping, and had him out hunting quite regularly during the winter, until he had settled down with us, and was quite happy in himself. Then we took him racing. I rode him quietly down to the start, but he refused to start on the starting line, and the others had gone fifteen to twenty lengths before I finally got him going. I let him canter slowly into the first fence and just popped him over. And I did that for the first three fences until he discovered that no one was caning him, no one was forcing him to do anything. And I sat still on him for the rest of the race. After we had gone about two miles, his own innate ability and superior quality got him up into fifth or sixth place in a field of twelve. I let him lie there quite happily for the next half mile until, as he was beginning to tire, I pulled him up.

We didn't run him the following Saturday, but a fortnight later I had him out again. And again I ran almost exactly the same race, except this time I let him finish, and we finished very comfortably and quietly in fourth place.

The third time out was Easter Monday. He jumped off at the start so sharply that he nearly had me out of the saddle, and I had great difficulty in restraining him and keeping him in the middle of the field. We did one complete circuit in the middle of the field. And then on the second circuit I just let him go. Unfortunately he fell at the last fence but one, when in the lead, or I think he would have won. He was a most unlucky horse, because shortly afterwards he broke down in one of his fore legs, and of course never raced again. But simply by letting him take his racing easy, and enjoy his jumping and galloping, what had previously been something to fear and dread, had become a terrific game, something he really enjoyed. This is what makes handling difficult horses such a joy: by the time you have finished with them you have completely changed their mental attitude and their outlook on life.

A further example of such a transformation took place in a horse called Ranne, sent to us one spring as unbreakable. Her owner had sent her away to the stallion and at the same time to be broken, but unfortunately the man who did it was rather rough with her, and she became completely unmanageable. When first I went into her loose box, she just stood in the corner and shook with fear.

So the first thing to do was to overcome her fear of men. My method was very simple. I didn't fuss or bother her in any way. I just left her alone, only going into her box when I fed her. The result was that within forty-eight hours she was looking for me to bring her food: she, who had been afraid of all men, was associating a man with her dinner. So she was calling for her dinner and calling me at the same time.

The next stage was also simple. When I gave her food, I stood by the basin until she was eating. And then I scratched her in an itchy place. All horses have places that itch: under the chin, on the line of the jaw; on the chest; or at the base of the neck just in front of the withers. Horses always like to be scratched in these places, so simply by scratching – in Ranne's case particularly the chest – I made her look forward to seeing me. From her chest I graduated to scratching her neck, from the wither up. And within two or three days I could run my hand up and down her neck, and scratch her behind her ears. The next stage was simply going in and out of her stable. Each time I went in I just scratched her. So within some ten days I had transformed a horse from exhibiting sheer terror at the sight of any man, into looking forward to seeing me – by doing absolutely nothing other than making the horse want me to go into her loose box, first because I fed her, then because I scratched her.

From then on her gentling went very quickly. She was an extremely sweet mare to gentle. The only thing that had to be watched was her tendency to anxiety, so each new experience had to be introduced very gradually, or she would get into a panic.

We started her off jumping low poles. She didn't really enjoy jumping them, but each time she jumped a fence I made a terrific fuss of her, and within a very short time jumping the fences became a reward in itself.

The important thing in gentling what had been an unmanageable horse was to make each task, when it was learned, the reward for doing the next task. The first task she had to learn was to accept me: then accepting me, and being made a fuss of by me, became the reward for being ridden, and jumped. And then the jumping became the reward for doing dressage work. And so it went on. If the presentation of each new thing is correct, then that will naturally become sufficient reward.

In fact, until she went back to her owner, I hunted hounds off Ranne for the first three months of the season, and she was one of the best hunters I have ever ridden. She was absolutely rock steady when I wanted her to stand still. On top of this, she was an extremely fast and willing horse, and she became a superb, but very careful, fencer.

It is fascinating to see how far this kind of learning, making each task when learned the reward for doing the next, can go from the original aim, and also to observe how long this kind of learning lasts. How can you explain why a horse should expend enormous effort on a task just because it was originally associated with praise? Most horses work just hard enough to avoid pain – that is to avoid being punished for not working. Yet a number of horses will work far beyond their limits for *no* apparent reason.

Why for example will a good steeple-chaser gallop himself to complete exhaustion? He doesn't do it from fear of pain – very often he will go on galloping and jumping long after he has lost his jockey. He doesn't do it to stay with other horses, because very often, after he has lost his jockey, he will lead by ten or twelve lengths.

Molfre was such a horse. At the third fence at the Carmarthen point-to-point, Molfre was brought down by another horse falling across him. I was knocked out for a moment or two, but when I came to, I could see Molfre pursuing the other horses. When he came into sight again out of the dip, he was ten lengths in front of the other horses. All the fences at Carmarthen on the far side of the course are island fences – that is to say they stand in the middle of the field, and the horse if he wants to can go around them. Yet Molfre, ten lengths in front of the other horses, met each fence right, and jumped it right. We eventually caught him when he had done almost a complete circuit by himself.

A horse who for no obvious reason will gallop himself completely into the ground is little Cefn Solomon. Cefn Solomon belonged to Dill Thomas of the Cefn Park Stud, and he had bought it for his daughter Bunny to hunt, and possibly to race at a later date. He asked me to ride him to begin with, so we introduced him to racing slowly. He went quite creditably, being placed in most races. Then in a very hard maiden race at the Glamorgan point-to-point I was asked to ride him again. I got a nice start and led into the first fence, to keep well out of the way of trouble, and I kept among the first two or three over the first half-mile. I eased him back to sixth or seventh place for the next two miles, and half a mile from home I was lying fifth. I could feel little Cefn Solomon was getting tired, so I just clicked my tongue, and, keeping him straight and balanced, let him go on at his own pace, encouraging him with my voice. The first two miles had been fast for most of the field, and they started dropping back past me. I still managed to keep my tiring horse straight, and placed him so that he could jump the fences with the minimum of effort. We came over the last fence in second place, about three lengths behind the tiring leader. I knew that if I touched Cefn Solomon with a stick, or shifted in any way, I would unbalance him completely, so I just sat still and kept him going with my voice. Eventually we were beaten at the winning post by only about two lengths, and I came in for some criticism from the less knowledgeable spectators, yet the little horse was so tired going back from the finish to the paddock that he could hardly walk, and when he got back to his loose box that night, he refused to eat his supper and he just lay down flat for the next twenty-four hours, refusing to get up even to eat. It is always a mystery to me, what makes a horse like this gallop himself to complete exhaustion. I hadn't hit him, or even kicked him with my heels. I just sat still. Yet he had galloped on, driven by his own indomitable spirit, and will to win.

And what is more, that extremely hard race in no way diminished little Solomon's desire to race in future, and give his best at every opportunity. Dill decided in 1975 to run him again the following season, and in the spring of 1976, he came down for a day's hunting to see what sort of a mess I was making of hunting a pack of hounds. After hunting we talked over the prospects for the coming season, and which horses he was racing, and he told me that Solomon was fitter than ever he had been. He thought that he might win a race early in the season. He never spoke a truer word in all his life.

At the Banwen Miners point-to-point on 21st February, although the weather was atrocious, we came to the second last fence. I had pegged the favourite's lead back from four lengths to two lengths. We jumped the second last fence, the favourite being so tired that he rolled very wide to one side and I went past him. Down the hill, when I was sitting absolutely still and not having to ride at all, the favourite made one despairing effort, but he was so tired he couldn't take off from the ground, and went base over apex. I went past the winning post a very easy and comfortable winner, with little Solomon as fresh as if he had hardly been out of his stable.

If I had used a stick on Solomon the previous spring, I would have had to punish him very severely to have beaten the favourite then – and even if I *had* belted the living daylights out of him, I don't think I would have won. For if he had had a very punishing race at the Glamorgan, he would probably never have run again. And he would certainly never have won a race afterwards. But by sitting still and never punishing him, I had made sure he retained his enthusiasm for racing. We hope now that he will go on and win other races in the future.

It is of course possible to win one race on a horse by beating the living daylights out of him. But there are very few horses who will take it a second time. They will simply never get themselves into a situation in which they are likely to be asked for the supreme effort.

This is why it is so important to teach a horse with patience and understanding: so that he *wants* to do what you want him to do. And this is what a learned positive goal is all about. Cefn Solomon's motivation could only have been the fact that he associated his galloping and jumping with enjoying himself. He loved the praise and appreciation he had got in his previous races, when he had given everything he had. It is only by teaching a horse in this way that you can achieve the ultimate in competition.

But learned positive goals have also to be constantly renewed. The horse has to receive praise and reward all the time, so that he learns to keep his enthusiasm. The success of little Cefn Solomon was maintained simply and solely because of the patience and understanding of his owner, Dill Thomas, and his daughter Bunny. Without these things, he would have been just another nice little lady's hunter.

To explain the fact that most horses work no harder than is required of them to avoid punishment, and others work quite happily without any obvious reward, requires however something more than the idea that they work for learned negative or positive goals. There is in fact a convergence of motives. This means simply that several reasons for doing something become involved in a single activity. To put it another way, one particular kind of work may lead to satisfaction of several needs at the same time.

Take the case of the green, untouched horse that becomes a superlative race horse or show jumper. He is like any other horse to begin with, he will learn either because he wants to do something, because he has damned well got to do it or get clobbered, or because if he does what he is told he gets praised. But as time goes on, he will begin to enjoy his work. He will begin to enjoy the burst of energy of jumping and racing. His training will keep him active and fit, and will satisfy his need for activity, excitement and movement. It will satisfy his somewhat restless nature by keeping both his body moving, and his mind alert. If he is a show-jumper the challenge and problems of jumping fences will satisfy his need to exercise his brain. He will also enjoy the praise and adulation that he gets when he wins or does well in a competition. So a whole variety of motives will converge with experience, re-inforcing each other and increasing his will to perform.

All these motives have then to be taken into account when training and handling a horse, because it is the fulfilment of as many as possible of the varying needs of the horse that makes the successful competitor. Without the right psychological make-up, physical excellence will go for nothing.

A friend of mine has for instance a very good hunter mare, with superb confirmation for a showjumper. She will jump five foot with ease but she is useless in competition. Time and time again she will do a clear round up to the last fence and then have the last fence down. In spite of her physical excellence Fred Broome had to decide that she would never make a showjumper, simply and solely because she didn't want to win in competition.

On the other hand, with the right mental approach a horse can make up for a certain amount of physical shortcoming in competition. An example of this is my wife's cob, Rostellan, or to give him his correct name, Trefaes Dafydd. As far as I know he is the only registered Welsh Cob taking part in one-day events. He is fifteen hands high, and like all Welsh cobs, his natural pace is a trot. Again like all Welsh cobs, whilst he can jump great heights, he has great difficulty in jumping spreads. So what drives him to gallop himself to exhaustion, or tackle cross-country in a one-day event? First of all my wife has had him for six years now, and he has developed such love for her that he will do any-thing to please her. And I have already described how, when he has misbehaved, he looks as crestfallen as a small boy who knows he is going to be punished for being naughty.

So the first and greatest need within him is the drive to please the person he loves most. And he achieves this by giving every-thing he has got. Then again he is very fit, and full of corn, so he has a great store of energy within him to be released by jumping and galloping. Again, like many Welsh cobs, he is a very great showman, and he enjoys the admiration he gets from what amounts to his fan club. So that whilst it is physically impossible for him ever to win a one-day event, simply and solely because no matter how much he tries he can't gallop fast enough to do so, every time he takes part he puts in an outstanding performance.

Probably the best performance he has ever put in was in spring 1976 at Penrice. After a season's hunting he was as fit as a fiddle, so, as often happens in one-day events, his very fitness meant that he didn't do a very good dressage test. But the show-jumping and cross-country were both extremely stiff. All the fences in the showjumping, and most of them in the cross-country, were absolute maximum for one-day events. (In fact two of the cross-country fences had to be made smaller, as they were over the maximum). The showjumping fences also included spreads, and were on a slope, which made jumping extremely difficult. Yet Rostellan did an outstanding round. How he managed to complete some of the spreads, which in theory were completely beyond him, I do not know. And again when it came to the cross-country he performed way beyond his natural ability. It was a very long and stiff course, with plenty of ups and downs. The first three fences were comparatively easy, the third fence being a spread of bales which he made nothing of since he got over his difficulty in jumping a big spread simply by jumping on top of the bales, and off them. Fences four and five were big crossed poles, and then a fence and ditch, and another fence out over it. He got over these perfectly well. There was a long stretch into the sixth fence, and he carted my wife flat-out, steadied himself and jumped the fence immaculately. He proceeded round the course at such speed that by the time he had got to the third last fence he was very tired. But his determination and spirit carried him over the finish. By then he was exhausted, having galloped himself into the ground in a time nearly as fast as that of the thoroughbreds.

Getting a horse fit for any competition is rather like stoking up a boiler until you have got the right head of steam to be released: too much steam and the boiler explodes, or the horse becomes unmanageable, and expends too much energy early on; too little steam, that is too little fitness and mental drive, and the horse won't compete at all. At the same time you are building up tension, which he releases by expending everything he has in the competition.

Over the course of years, by careful training, the horse will have been taught to love jumping, or whatever he is doing. And that's another reason for competing well. Any competition horse is a very proud horse, and also a terrific showman, so the admiration he receives when he is competing satisfies him, and the praise and admiration he receives when he does well gives him an added incentive to excel himself.

Thus in competition as in any form of riding, the greater the number of motivations you can involve in the experience, the greater the pleasure you and the horse will get out of it. Though I tend to emphasize competition and jumping, these of course are not the whole purpose of riding, or even the major parts of it: they are with us, as with most people, only a very small part of our work with horses. Most of the time we are just hacking, and schooling. But the advantage of competition is that it provides you with a measure of whether the work you are doing on the horse is correct. If each time you compete with a horse, the horse does a little better, then you know that your schooling and basic work is correct. If on the other hand the horse is making no progress, or appears to be going backwards when you are competing, then you know that the work you are doing is wrong. So competition is a very necessary yardstick for any form of equestrianism. And of course unless your schooling and riding have some object in view, they tend to lack point and become boring. If on the other hand you are aiming for something particular – a showjumping competition or a dressage competition, a one-day event, a race or a day's hunting – your schooling and training will take on a new urgency, and stimulate the horse accordingly.

Rostellan may take part in two or three showjumping com-

Horses are herd animals, so they tend to graze together, and move on together. Herd of ponies grazing loose on the mountain

The herd has a leader – often one of the older mares. If she moves, the others follow

They are sociable animals – with each other, and with man. Here CARAVAN & ANDY say 'hello' to each other in the stable-yard

CUDDLES shows his affection
for the author by mouthing
his hands

IANTELLA saying 'I Like You'

Joined by CUDDLES

Aggression in horses: the herd leader, REES, gives a young
upstart a nip to keep him in his place

IANTELLA threatens ANDY

ANDY backs away in fear. Note the ears laid back angrily in all the pictures

Horses need movement, and stimulation. CUDDLES has been kept in the stable too long, and as soon as he is let loose, he trots down the road to get rid of excess energy

CUDDLES shows his restlessness by 'bouncing' under his rider

Horses are curious – they come up to investigate their master's prone figure – hoping he's dead, suggests author

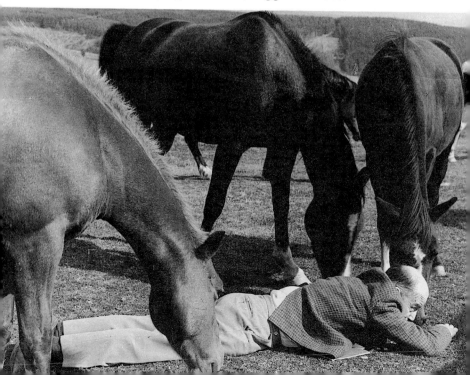

CUDDLES searches the author's daughter-in-law JUDY's pocket to see what she has in it

WATCH expressing annoyance and suppressed exuberance – note the ears twitching and muscles tense

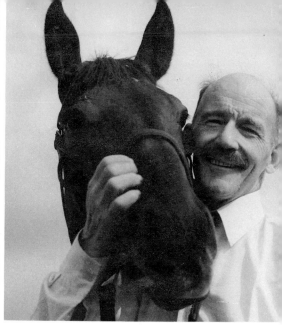

Top Left: The author's understanding of his horses' needs and feelings can be put to good use in training. The need for food and drink suggests a reward
Top Right: Scratching fingers – another reward. WATCH shows his appreciation
Below: CUDDLES has misbehaved and flees to safety to escape retribution

The horse's need to be with other horses is here used to teach TRABOLGAN to jump – he follows CUDDLES over small fences

The horse's love of excitement and need for stimulation can be expressed in competitiveness with other horses – WATCH and IANTELLA racing over a fence

RIDING A HORSE FOR THE FIRST TIME

The author reassures and restrains CARAVAN

He accustoms CARAVAN to walking with a rope halter dropped round his neck, leading him at the same time with a bucket of nuts

Once CARAVAN is used to a halter, the author slips a bridle over his head

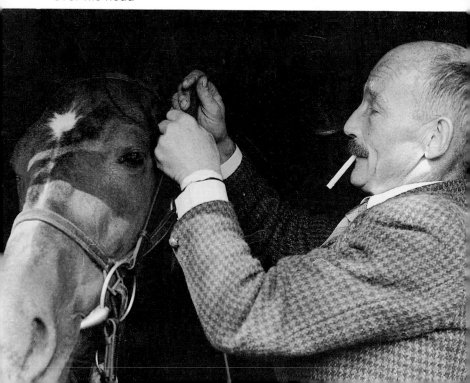

Then while CARAVAN has his nose in a bucket of feed, he leans over him, gets a leg up, and mounts

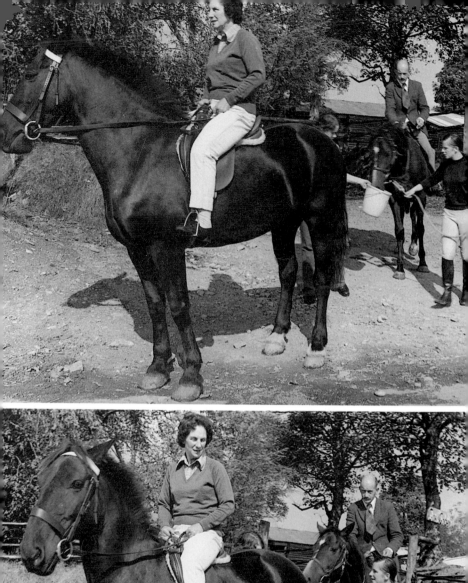

The author, on the new horse, encourages him to leave the yard by getting his wife, on another horse, to lead the way. The bucket of feed is still there, so the horse is being motivated not only by his need to please his master, but also by his need for food, and his need for the company of other horses

The horse follows the bucket of feed, allowing himself to be ridden without a companion

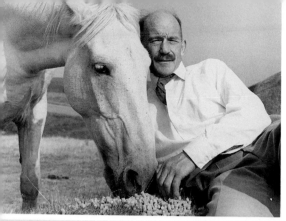

Henry Blake with REES

With COBBLERS and REES (Centre)

Riding WATCH (Lower)

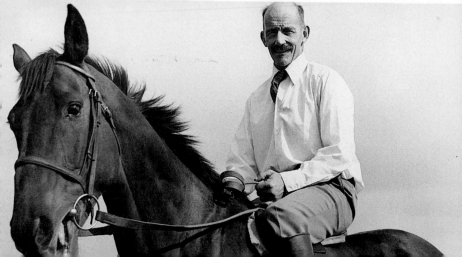

REWARD AND PUNISHMENT 97

petitions, a couple of hunt trials and a couple of one-day events in the whole year, though he will also have twenty or thirty days' hunting. But we can see by each one-day event and by each showjumping competition and each hunter trial, whether Rostellan is fit and well. Because whilst he may be jumping out of his skin at home and in the box, you can really only tell whether the horse is right and well when it comes to the crunch of competition.

We like also to vary the competitions which our horses take part in, simply and solely because each competition needs a different form of schooling and work. Each small riding club competition he takes part in, because he has had special schooling for that competition, makes for a slightly better and more widely experienced horse.

In short, I tend to look at any races, hunter trials or one-day events I take part in rather as a schoolmaster looks on the end-of-term examinations: I use them as a measure of progress the horse has made in the intervening time. As well as telling me whether the horse is fit enough, and well enough, they tell me whether the form of training I have been giving him is correct.

6: *Using the Horse's Natural Drives*

If you look out of your window, you may see a tree, a motor car and a dog. You will know that they are a tree, a motor car and a dog because they are similar in appearance and behaviour to objects that you have seen before that are trees, motor cars and dogs. You will know that the tree will stay where it is, the dog will walk and bark, and the motor car will smell, make a horrible noise and, if you are lucky, get you from point A to point B. Experience has taught you to recognize objects and predict their behaviour, so you act accordingly.

The horse organizes his experience in much the same way. If you have been feeding him horse and pony nuts, and change him to race-horse nuts, or Olympic nuts, he will eat them because they are similar to the food he has been eating before. In the same way, when you are riding or jumping him, he will treat various objects and tasks according to how he can relate them to something that he has done before. He will jump a variety of objects and perform a variety of tasks quite happily and readily. provided only that each is similar to something he has done before. And most of your training makes use of this fact.

If, for example, a horse has been accustomed to jumping a single pole two feet high, and you put a second pole underneath it, he will jump it quite happily because jumping two poles is very little different from jumping one pole. If you put the second pole parallel to the first, say a foot or two away from the first, again he will jump it quite happily. He will relate anything new to something he has done previously, and provided his original experience has been pleasant, he will be quite happy to attempt the new one. But if the thing he has done before has been unpleasant, he will treat anything similar with suspicion.

For nearly two years we had Madam on the place. She was rather an antisocial horse to the rest of the herd, so much so that if any other horse went near her, she kicked its teeth in. I then bought a nice little black mare at Llanybyther horse sale because she was something similar in appearance to Madam, and the same type. Since we had done very well with Madam, I bought the little mare hoping that she would be as good. When we turned her out with the other horses, all the other horses gave her a very wide berth for four or five days – she was similar in appearance to Madam, who had kicked them, so they treated Beauty (that is what we called her) in exactly the same way. The way I guess they thought was: she is like Madam; Madam kicks; therefore she kicks. And until they found that Beauty had a much sweeter and kinder nature than Madam, they kept well away from her.

This logic by association is also illustrated by my experience with my beloved twelve-two pony Jezebel, whom I have already described. She is an extremely intelligent, active and rather nervous pony with a fantastic jump in her, but the temper of a demon. I got her as an eight-year-old. Her previous owner persuaded me by threatening that if I didn't take her he would have her shot in the field the next day, she was such a nuisance in making his other horses as impossible to catch as she was. Even after I had had her for some time, she would jump five-foot gates with ease rather than be caught. On one occasion she jumped a four-foot barbed wire fence with a ten-foot drop on the other side, without turning a hair.

Her temper and her determination not to be confined, combined with the fear learned through the ill treatment she had received, expressed itself in Jezebel in a hatred of all mankind. Men to her were unpleasant, brutal and to be escaped from. If she couldn't escape, she attacked them – not because she wanted to attack them, but because it was the only way she knew of defending herself.

It is of course impossible to change the attitudes and habits of a lifetime in five minutes. And in an eight-year-old mare of the calibre of Jezebel, you can never completely get rid of old suspicions. But what I had to try to do was gradually to replace her negative associations with the idea of man, with good ones. I had consistently to offer her kindness and gentleness, and persuade her to associate good things with me. And hard work and great patience have at last built between her and me a very great affection and a very deep trust each of the other. I still can't, and I don't ever think I will be able to, walk up to her in the field and catch her without difficulty. But when I open the gate of the field she'll trot a mile down the road and into a stable, and stand there waiting to be tied up. Funnily enough the odd time when I have come off her hunting or in competition, she has stood waiting for me to catch her and get on again.

We can't of course *know* how a horse associates one experience with another, since we can't experience what a horse experiences. The only thing we can do, is to infer that since he reacts the same way to two similar foods, to him they appear and taste the same. Or if he jumps two fences in the same way, that they appear the same to him. If a horse has been friendly with a cat and used to having it in his loose box, and when a dog walks into his box he treats the dog in the same way that he treats the cat, it is reasonably safe to assume that he is relating his experience with the cat to his attitude to the dog.

As in everything else with the psychology of a horse, we can only infer the horse's motives from his reactions. But our observation of these reactions does lead us to conclude that one of the experiences most readily generalized by the horse is that of fear.

If a horse tries very hard to please his owner or rider, he may very well be motivated by fear, if his original trainer was difficult to please and rather cruel.

A horse may jump a fence out of desire to please his owner, because he enjoys jumping fences, or because he knows if he doesn't he will have the living daylight whaled out of him. But motives may also be in conflict: the horse's desire to jump a fence and please his rider may conflict with the fear of hurting himself if he does so – or even with his tendency to pure laziness!

A horse in competition and jumping is very often subject to this conflict of motive. You might, at a fence, get four motives all in conflict: a desire to please his rider, in conflict with a desire not to hurt himself, and his wish not to expend more energy than he has to, in turn in conflict with the fear of being punished. These drives are not always in balance: if the fear of hurting himself is very great, and his desire to please his rider very small, he will refuse to jump the fence. Or if his desire not to expend energy again is very large, and his fear of being hit is very small, again he will refuse.

As an experiment, we took Madam and put her in a small dressage competition with two different riders on her, the second one going *hors du concours*. They were both judged by the same judge. The first rider had a dressage score of eighty-nine penalties; but the second rider had a score of just forty-eight penalties. The difference in the score was simply accounted for by the difference in the horse's desire to please. We chose Madam because she tends to be particularly nappy, and whilst a very active little mare has to be ridden with a minimum contact on the reins, or she throws her head about. The difference in the score was not in the competence of the riders, for both were good riders. However, Madam didn't get on with the first girl on her back, and she adored the second. So it was a pretty fair test of how desire to please can change the performance of the horse.

There are of course other environmental factors affecting a horse's performance on any particular occasion. If for example he is undernourished, his desire to conserve energy will far outweigh his fear of punishment. If on the other hand the horse is overfed, and under-exercised, he will be so bubbling with energy that he will jump a fence and gallop, whether his rider wishes to or not. We try to see that all such factors are working for us when we deal with our horses, and in particular we lay very great emphasis on our horses enjoying themselves: partly because we like our horses, but mainly because we know that if a horse wants to do something, it is so much easier to get him doing it than if he doesn't.

In our training we try to relate high levels of performance with high levels of enjoyment. At the same time we realize that over-indulgence, that is letting a horse do what he wants to, to mis-behave as he wants to, is not kindness, it's just another form of ill-treatment, even when from the best of motives. If for example you allow a horse to get away with biting you, without punching his teeth in, he will bite anybody and everyone, and he will certainly come to a stage when he is biting you so much that you have to get rid of him. And a horse that bites people has only one end: that's in a Cat's Meat tin.

Over-indulgence of a horse, and allowing him to acquire vices, in short, is not only not kindness, it can even amount to extreme cruelty. For it must always be remembered that many of the things that a horse does, he does spontaneously and uncon-sciously – it is you, the rider, who must do some of his thinking for him and decide where his best interests are.

Rostellan, for example, as I have already said, will eat whatever you put in front of him. No matter how much you give him, he will go on eating, for he is a compulsive feeder. This, in part any-way, is because he was very badly treated as a foal and as a young horse. If anything, since we have had him, he's been slightly over-fed. Yet if he is allowed to, he will eat nine or ten pounds of corn at a sitting, and no matter how much hay you give him, it will always be cleared up by the morning.

The scientists tell us, and no doubt they are right, that the horse's stomach can carry only five pounds of food. But on two measure trials, Rostellan ate first nine-and-a-half pounds of horse and pony nuts, and in the second a whole bale of hay, which weighed thirty-nine pounds: between six o'clock one evening, and eight-thirty the following morning, he had eaten all that hay, and on top of that he had eaten five-and-a-quarter pounds of horse and pony nuts! His normal day's feed was fifteen pounds of horse and pony nuts, and ten pounds of hay.

This is the sort of phenomenon that makes for difficulty in trying to understand horses! For if you were to be able to ask Rostellan why he ate so much, he would probably say because he was hungry. But of course this cannot be so, since he goes on eating long after he has been adequately fed. It is probably in his case a legacy of a certain amount of underfeeding when he was young. But compulsive eating isn't always traceable to malnutrition when a horse was young: I have seen a four-month-old foal so grossly fat that it was suffering from lamenitis; and I have also come across horses that have been almost starved, yet have been very difficult to get into condition because, in spite of being underfed, they remain very shy feeders.

A horse, like a human being, will acquire habits of which he is largely unaware. He has been conditioned by his experience, and often one can do no more than guess at that experience.

For instance, a horse may shy at a certain place on the road, for no reason that is apparent at the time. At some time in the past, let us say, he was frightened badly there. When he passed the same place the following day, the memory of being frightened there was still with him, so he shied again at the same spot. And again on the third day. Within a week or two, unless great care had been taken with him, he would have acquired the habit of shying at a certain spot. If he changed hands and went past the same spot again he would still shy there, and the new owner wouldn't know the reason why. Indeed, if a horse gets used to shying in one place, he may start shying in another, again for no apparent reason, and he acquires the bad habit of shying simply and solely because of a frightening experience that was not dealt with at the time it occurred.

One horse I had some time ago had the intriguing habit of moving his tail to one side when he dunged – he didn't raise his tail to dung as a horse normally does, he just moved it to one side. When I tried to trace this habit back, I discovered that he had been very badly fed, and got into an extremely weak condition at one period when he was a two-year-old. The effort of lifting his tail to dung had been just too much for him, so he had learned merely to move his tail to one side. Even when he got stronger – he was jumping out of his skin when we had him – he still retained the habit of moving his tail in this way.

Thus, since the horse is a creature of habit, it is extremely important to stop him acquiring bad habits, and to make sure that he acquires good ones.

I have a friend who hunts a lot, and when out hunting she always trots up to a fence to make sure that it is jumpable. As a result, all her horses have acquired the habit of refusing once at every fence: solely because she does the very sensible thing of making sure that each fence is free of wire before jumping it. It means that none of her horses will jump in competition.

Kerry, when he came to us, had the reputation of striking out with his front feet. He didn't. What he did was bounce up and down on his front feet, and this had terrorized his previous owner so much that as soon as Kerry bounced she jumped to one side. So he had got into the habit of 'bouncing' whenever he wanted to get past anyone – a very threatening habit indeed. When he came to us, we cured him of this very quickly. But what he did was simply transfer the habit to his jumping. When we were hunting, just before he started into a fence, he would bounce up and down on his front feet. Just as he had bounced when trying to pass his owner, who was a barrier, he bounced in front of a fence because this was another barrier. This is a perfect example of how a habit once acquired can be transferred to a completely different situation, long after the original reason has been forgotten.

This brings up the question of measuring motives. When you have discovered what makes a horse do something, it is often important to know just how strong the motive for doing it is. But you can't measure it with a tape measure, nor put it on a scale and conclude that this motive is two feet high, and weighs three and a half pounds. It is possible however to measure a motive, or rather to measure its strength. This can be done in four ways.

First we can measure certain drives according to what the horse *consumes* as a result of his drive: you can measure the strength of his thirst by the amount of water he will drink, or the amount of food a horse will eat will measure his hunger. You can also measure the greed of a horse using this method.

This you do, having fed the horse sufficient corn for his needs, by measuring the amount of food he will eat on top of that. This is the way we measured Rostellan's greed. His normal feed was five pounds, but in our first test he ate nine-and-a-half pounds of corn at a single feed.

Biddy, on the other hand, whose normal feed is six pounds three times a day, would not only not eat seven pounds when we offered it, but she wouldn't eat her next feed either. So we can say that Biddy's greed is nil, whilst Rostellan's is ninety percent.

Another method of measuring a need is to deprive the horse. This is a good method for measuring such factors as the amount of movement or the amount of light a horse requires.

The need for movement and light, which are vitally necessary for a horse's mental and physical wellbeing – if he is deprived of either he will not only become mentally unbalanced, but he will also lose condition physically as quickly as if he were dying of starvation – cannot be measured directly. But they can be measured indirectly by measuring the effect of withdrawal of either. Measuring the effect of withdrawal of movement is best done with a horse that is being stabled at night and out by day. A reasonably active and alert horse, if you turn him out into a field after being in at night, will canter round a couple of times and then settle down and graze. This particular trial, to eliminate a build-up effect, we normally carry out once a week for three or four weeks. It is quite simple to do: you measure the time it takes the horse to settle down and graze after being turned out over a period of days. And then one night, instead of putting him into a loose box, you tie him up in a very narrow stall to restrict his movements, for twelve hours, then you turn him out the following day and measure the time it takes for him to settle down and graze. By subtracting the average time it takes him normally to settle down to graze, from the average of three or four occasions when he has been allowed only minimal movement at night, you can measure the effect the restriction of movement has had on him. If the average time it takes him to settle down grazing normally on being turned out is four and a half minutes, but on the four occasions when he had been restricted in movement it was seven and a half minutes, the difference would be a hundred and eighty seconds. We simply call this a movement factor of a hundred and eighty. And by doing this with three or four horses, we can compare the different amounts of movement and exercise various horses need.

These figures, when it comes to applying them in training, are usually in *inverse* ratio to the amount of exercising a horse requires. That is, a horse that takes a relatively long time to settle down after a night of restricted movement, is likely to have taken more exercise in his loose box than one who takes a short time to settle down after a night of restricted movement. So it is the horse that moves little in his loose box during the night that in fact needs most exercising by day.

Another way to measure the strength of a horse's drive is to test exactly what he will do, or how far he will go, in order to satisfy it. If, for instance, a horse will perform very highly for praise, and you know that he will improve his performance through praise, you know that his desire for praise is very strong. If on the other hand a horse will improve after a clout with a stick, then you know that his fear of punishment is strong. By a series of small trials you can test which form of stimulus will make your horse perform most willingly, and which are his strongest drives.

The fourth way of measuring, a variation on the last which is extremely important in training a horse, is to test just what a horse will learn to do in order to attain a particular object.

For example, when we are schooling a horse to jump, we plan the routine so that the last thing the horse does before going home is to jump. He thus very quickly associates going home to his dinner with jumping. And of course we jump towards home. So the horse very quickly learns that if he jumps the fence that he is pointed at, then he goes home. Whereas if he messes about, refuses, and knocks the fence all over the place, he has another half hour to forty minutes work before him. We measure the strength of his wish to go home by the way he jumps the fences when he knows that he is going home, compared with his performance, say, before he goes out to work.

The fascination about horses of course is that no two of them are the same, and their personalities vary even from day to day. Indeed the whole character of a horse can alter once his personality is allowed to develop, and one of my greatest joys is to watch the change in a sullen and rather bad tempered horse when his personality starts to grow.

Few horses have given me more pleasure in this way than Charlie. We had bought Charlie at Ascot in the autumn, with three possible aims in view: to put him in one-day eventing, to ride him point-to-pointing, or to put him into training for hurdling. What I had not intended with Charlie was that he would do very much hunting. His breeding makes him a six-furlong flat-race horse, and I didn't think that he would stand up to very much hunting, though we used him hunting a little, simply to get him interested in his work.

But unfortunately for me, Ranne's owner came back from America and naturally wanted Ranne back to hunt herself, so Charlie was pressed into service as my second horse, which meant that two days a month I had to hunt hounds off him. And this Charlie didn't enjoy to start with.

First, he didn't like the hounds. Second, he hated being by himself. And third, he didn't like the work involved because it meant galloping down hills, which he thought was extremely dangerous. So he was a bad hunter. But very slowly, in spite of himself, he developed a liking for the job. Once he discovered that the hounds weren't going to bite him or eat him alive, he stopped taking umbrage every time my hounds came near me. And then he began to enjoy hunting, with my daughter Paddy riding him on the days he needed a day's hunting, and I didn't need him. Next he began to enjoy jumping. He realized that scrambling fences and pig netting and banks, which are the greater part of the obstacles we jump out hunting here, were quite fun to jump. He also began to enjoy showing himself off at the Meet, leading all the horses all the time. This development of his pride was easy to see in the way he began to hold his head up, and stick his tail out at an angle of sixty degrees like an Arab stallion. He absolutely swaggered out of town after a Meet. But he still wasn't enjoying the hard work involved in drawing, and he certainly didn't like being by himself when galloping with running hounds.

But suddenly all this changed. We had an extremely good hunt. It started off with a very sharp point of about a mile and a half in which he was being his usual Bolshie self, then, when the fox left the second cover, he got away a bit in front of hounds, and as we often do I went one way and my wife went the other – in case we got stopped by an unjumpable barbed wire fence. I hunted hounds slowly for about half a mile on Charlie. Charlie was still going forwards backwards, and eventually we came to a boundary fence that was impossible. So, I got off my horse, left him standing by the fence, and went on hunting hounds on foot. Shortly after, my wife came up. I took her horse off her, and she had to take Charlie the long way round and catch up with me again. This took about half an hour, and Charlie was absolutely furious. He has got a very nasty habit, when he is very angry, of doing little fly kicks, which are uncomfortable to ride, and he had done this the whole time my wife was on him. When she caught us up again the fox was in a patch of kale, and we were trying to get him out. So I changed back on to Charlie, and she took her horse. Charlie was completely different: he was suddenly putting his heart into his work. His whole attitude had changed, from that of a reluctant partner to that of someone who was doing his best in what he thought were impossible circumstances.

Hounds came out of the kale like rockets, and as they went over a wire boundary fence and disappeared from view, we lost them completely. And so the first whip, my wife and I went looking for them. We all made wrong guesses at the direction in which they had gone, and spent the next hour going round in ever increasing circles, until Grayling, the horse my wife was riding, could go no further. And Charlie too was extremely tired. But poor Charlie had to go on, because I had to find the hounds, and we had another ten miles to go. I was expecting ten miles of hell, because Charlie would be by himself which he hated. But not a bit of it. Charlie gave everything he had and went happily and willingly. Even when we eventually found hounds, we had a six-mile hack back to the Meet with them, yet although Charlie was as tired as he possibly could be, he went home with his ears pricked and his tail up. When at last he saw the trailer he let out a wicker of delight, and couldn't get into it fast enough – a horse who in the past had been somewhat awkward to load.

After that Charlie put all he could into his hunting. I think what had happened was first, that he had suddenly seen *why* he was supposed to be doing the things that I was asking him to do, and second, when I changed on to my wife's horse, that he thought he had been demoted and was in disgrace, so he was extremely relieved when I got back on him and he discovered that he had been promoted again – though why he should think he was being demoted when my wife got on him, I don't know, because she is much kinder and sympathetic a rider than I am when I am hunting hounds. My horse has to go, whether he is tired or not, simply because you have to stay with hounds when you are hunting them. She nurses her horse, and looks after him, whereas anything I'm hunting has to look after itself and me.

Charlie, in effect, wanted status and approval, and by offering him both we had changed his whole attitude to hunting. His story shows how important it is to know what a horse's needs and desires are, and how strong they are, so that we can know how far we can go in using his existing desires to make him want to do something new.

I've seen a very nervous filly walk up and down next to a rail six inches high, rather than step over it to get to her food, which was a mere two yards the other side of the rail. Later on the same filly was tearing at her bit to jump three-foot-six fences. The only difference in the filly, other than a certain amount of fitness, was that she had learned to *want* to jump fences.

Hunger and thirst are controlled by factors from within the body. But other factors also have a great influence on needs as primary as these, and we have already seen that they vary from one horse to another.

A horse, for example, will often drink water that it doesn't need. If when you are out riding, you allow him, he will sip at a pool of water, then fifty or a hundred yards further on stop and sip at another pool of water. A horse that has been recently fed will still eat a handful of nuts, and pick at the grass in the hedgerow if allowed to. This is partly because most horses have a natural instinct to consume as much as possible to store up body fat against a time of need, and partly because eating can relieve nervous tension. We have discovered that after a race, a horse will cool down and relax more quickly if allowed to stop every few yards and take a mouthful of grass while he is being walked.

Sexual and maternal drives too are no more constant in horses than in man. During her natural cycle the hormone balance in a mare's blood alters completely, so the very nature of the horse alters. This may have a considerable bearing upon her performance: it is well established that a mare in season usually races well below her normal level of ability. On the other hand there are some mares who will win races only when they are in season. And since hormone balance has a bearing upon a mare's racing performance, it is probable that it will also affect her performance at showjumping, or eventing, and any other form of competition:

in fact, that a mare's performance and ability will vary right through the twenty-one-day cycle. If you drew a graph of her performance at competition through a period of weeks, it would almost certainly bear a direct relation to a graph of her sexual cycle. In some mares the highest point of performance is at the mid-point between the two heat periods.

Towards the end of a mare's pregnancy other hormones come into play. The presence of the foetus in the uterus stimulates production of prolactin in the pituitary glands. And though no experimental work has been done on this phenomenon in mares, some experiments on rats are extremely interesting. Virgin female rats put in contact with baby rats, even though they had not bred themselves, displayed typical maternal behaviour. And *the level of prolactin in their blood* at the end of a week was treble the normal level. If exposing mares to foals alters the hormones in their bodies too, it explains why one mare will act as a foster mother or an aunt to a foal: the sight of the foal actually induces changes in the hormones of the blood. Equally a mare will mother and protect an immature yearling, or a two- or three-year-old. She may even take a weak gelding under her wing. It also explains why some mares will look after their owners with maternal care, be the owner male or female; pony mares will often seem to look on their young owners as rather badly brought up foals!

The sexual drive in geldings varies quite considerably: from nil to a drive comparable with that of an uncastrated stallion. Pudding, who had served mares when he was young, before he was castrated, will even now serve a mare in season. A gelding's sex drive is affected by the age of castration, and the degree of sexual development at castration. The sexual drive in a gelding is very often expressed in extreme protectiveness towards his owner, if the owner is a woman. And the gelding tends to retain the protective instinct of a stallion for his mares.

Stallions themselves vary considerably in sexual drive: we actually had one stallion sent to us who wouldn't bother at all to serve mares that were in season. And we cured him. First, we changed his diet. Then we allowed him to run with single mares as they came into season, turning the mare out with him at least a week before she was due. His interest in mares gradually returned, and he is now serving very successfully.

7: *Sensory Stimulation*

If you observe horses carefully you can hardly escape the conclusion that, although some of their behaviour springs from their primary physical needs – for food, drink and sex – most is caused by something else altogether. You have only to watch a horse in his loose-box with the top part of the door open, standing most of the day with his head leaning out, watching what goes on outside, to realize that he has a great need for sensory stimulation: in other words that the horse needs to use his sight, his hearing, and his senses of touch, smell and taste. Leaning out of his stall, he can see us going to and from the house doing our daily chores, hear the sounds of what is going on in the countryside, smell the galaxy of odours that pervade the yard – of the dung heap, the hounds, the hay in the feeding house.

Without this stimulation for his senses, the horse is mentally deprived. We know from our own observations that if in a stall a horse is unable to see and hear what is going on outside, he will become depressed, will go off his food, and begin to deteriorate physically.

We have done two small experiments on this kind of deprivation. The first was on Molfre. He lived in the end loose box of the stable block where he could see and hear everything that was going on, and he spent his day, no matter what the weather, with his head out over the door, watching our comings and goings from the house, noting when we went out in the car, in which direction we went, and how long we were gone. When we came back he would welcome me back with a wicker of welcome. And each time I went past his stable door he would nudge me on the arm to say hello.

However, that January the weather was so terrible – there was a strong south-east wind, a mixture of Arctic gale, rain and sleet, all blowing into the front of the stable – that to stop Molfre getting frostbite in his ears I kept the top half of his door shut for three days. At the end of those three days he had changed dramatically. From his normal cheerful self, he had become morose and dejected, and his food consumption had dropped by over two pounds of corn per day. Yet as soon as we opened the door again, within twenty-four hours he was back to normal and his food consumption had risen again.

The horse also seems to have an emotional drive to take risks. He needs excitement, and this need is linked with his curiosity. You can see it for yourself if you keep a horse shut in a darkened stable for twenty-four hours, completely deprived of excitement and interest. When he comes out he will react to all sorts of objects, which normally he would ignore in passing, and exhibit alarm where in normal circumstances he would show none. This suggests a need for excitement, for fear as a stimulation, whether actual or imaginary. A horse will look for danger and excitement even when there is none there – which is what we have called the need for risk. And what we term boredom in horses is actually a deprivation, a failure to satisfy its need for stimulation and excitement.

This also we found with Molfre. When I took him out on the fourth day after he had been shut in, instead of just putting his head down and walking, as he does normally, he was jumping out of his skin. He shied six times on a five-hundred-yard stretch. It was a simple matter of reasoning to deduce that some change was affecting him, and the obvious change was the closed stable door. To check this theory, I had only to count the number of times the other horses shied in similar circumstances.

We found that over a stretch of road about five hundred yards, four horses between them shied twenty-one times – that is, an average of five times each. We then worked them for three days. Then over the next week we kept count of the number of times they shied on the same stretch of road – which they had been going up and down on for the previous twelve months – and we discovered that on an average they were shying half a time each: that is, over a week, the four horses between them shied sixteen times. After being shut up without any mental stimulation for four days, in other words, they had shied ten times as often as their average when being worked normally. This is a simple piece of research that could be carried out by anyone.

We concluded from our experiment that depriving the horses of any interest or excitement for four days caused them to look for interest and excitement, to manufacture things to be frightened of, in order to feed a need that had been building up within them.

The second experiment was in part also an involuntary one. Due to the bad summer of 1974, we were very short of good quality hay for the winter, and unable to get any more, so just before Christmas we changed over from corn and hay to complete horse food. The horses did extremely well physically – in fact they were fitter and better than they had ever been – but the effect on them mentally was quite unforeseen. Within twenty-four hours, they all became slightly edgy in temper and almost simultaneously they started eating the wooden stable partitions and doors. Their tempers were in a state very similar to my own when I am deprived of cigarettes for any length of time.

To satisfy their obvious need for something to chew, we eventually collected fir branches and gorse which we hung in their stables. These they could chew to their hearts' content while they were getting all the nutrients they needed in the complete horse food. But before we solved the problem this way, we did a little test. To measure their need for chewing, we creosoted all the wooden edges that the horses could chew. After one creosoting, two of the six horses stopped chewing altogether. Three of them stopped eating wood after two creosotings. But Biddy, who was having more food than any of the others (she was getting twenty-one pounds of complete horse food a day), was still chewing at the edge of the doors and partitions, after three coatings of creosote. I had to stop here, because she was beginning to get blisters on her mouth.

When we came to analyze these results, we found that although

Biddy, who had the greatest need to chew, was the horse receiving the most horse nuts per day, she was however the one
receiving least hay – only five to six pounds. And we also found
that the most placid horses were the ones who stopped chewing
the partitions first. Biddy was the most irritable and temperamental of them all, and the one who kept chewing longest. Once
we had supplied them with the fir tree tops and gorse to chew
at, all the horses' temperaments went back to normal.

I encountered the most extreme case I have seen of the effects
of sensory deprivation on a horse some twenty-five years ago in
Ireland. I was asked to take on a fifteen-three thoroughbred
gelding called Danny Boy, apparently completely unmanageable
and unbreakable, to try to break him. In his attempt to master
him, his owner had first deprived him of water. When this
hadn't worked he had tried shutting him in a darkened stable, and
when I was brought in he had been in a dark stable without light
or much fresh air for nearly a month. He had almost gone round
the bend. There he was, standing with his head near the ground,
shaking it, waving it from side to side for hours on end. His coat
was dull, he was extremely thin, and his staring eyes gave him
the appearance of being completely insane. When anyone opened
the stable door, he came at them with his teeth and his front
legs.

It took me nearly two and a half hours to get a halter on.
Eventually I managed it, attached a longer rope to the halter
rope, and opened the door and let him out into the cow yard.
Once he was outside, he galloped round and round for nearly half
an hour before finally he slowed to a trot. I had great difficulty
in making him change direction every five or ten minutes, since
I didn't want him galloping in the same direction for too long.
When he finally settled down to a walk, I managed to get him
into a much larger box, out of which he could see, and then for
the next forty-eight hours, I spent as much time as I could talking to him and making friends. Every day for the next fortnight,
I led him out for an hour or so, letting him wander at my side as
he wanted to, picking the grass. All the time I was talking to

him, and getting him settled. And after that it was quite simple. I lived at that time about fifteen miles from where he was stabled, and to save the long journey backward and forward I decided to shift him nearer to where I was living. I led him the first mile and a half of the journey, then I just popped on his back and rode the last thirteen and a half miles bareback, on a halter.

His advance from here was quite dramatic. He was never mad, of course, he had merely been handled roughly and been terrified. And the combination of rough handling, starvation, water-deprivation and being confined to a darkened stable, had temporarily unbalanced him. But once the need to have his senses stimulated had been satisfied, and he had been induced to relax in the company of human beings, he became an extremely easy and willing horse.

However, ten days after I got him near home, I had still not yet managed to get a saddle on his back. It was still one of the things of which he was terrified. So I was riding him without a saddle, with only a bridle, when one morning, to make a change in his work, I thought it might be a good idea to let him see hounds. I rode him towards where I knew hounds were hunting, and as I rode along the road, heard them find in a piece of gorse just above me. Then suddenly, without any warning, the fox popped out about five yards in front of me, followed hard by the whole pack. I turned Danny Boy into the bank, and he went over it like a stag: the first fence he had ever jumped in his life. Then ensued what was probably one of the best hunts I have ever had. Hounds ran absolutely straight for about fifteen miles, and we were stopped by wire only once during the day. Towards the end Danny was going so well that twice I jumped off a bank over barbed wire. We were very, very fortunate. Hounds were not going so fast that we couldn't stay with them, but on the other hand they never stopped hunting, eventually killing about fifteen miles from home. Danny, who until the start of the hunt had never jumped a fence, was within four or five fields of hounds all the time.

And then followed the most uncomfortable three hours I can

remember. After riding fifteen miles of cross-country without a saddle, my backside was like a piece of raw beef. And I was faced with a fifteen-mile hack home! I was so sore that it was absolutely agony even to walk, so for most of the way home I rode leaning across him on my stomach, until I had taken all the skin off my belly as well, and then I alternated between lying on my stomach and sitting on my backside for the last four miles. After I had groomed and watered Danny, I went home and had a bath, and spent the next forty-eight hours swathed in bandages trying to find the least agonizing place to lie on. But it was a fantastic hunt and worth every twinge of pain I suffered afterwards. And Danny Boy from that day on became a really wonderful hunter, and only two days after that first hunt I put a saddle on him without any trouble whatsoever.

There has been very little scientific work done, as far as I know, on deprivation in horses. But considerable work has been done on sensory deprivation in man and ape.

Twenty-odd years ago an American researcher named Buxton did an experiment on depriving human beings of all sensory stimulation. College students were paid twenty dollars a day – then quite a large amount of money – to lie on a comfortable bed, confined in a small, darkened and totally silent cubicle. To reduce visual stimulation to the minimum, all the students wore opaque goggles, and to reduce tactile stimulation they wore gloves on their hands and socks on their feet. At the beginning it seemed to the students that this was a very easy way to make money. But very quickly most of them found it intolerable. After two or three days they wanted nothing more than to get out. They began to have hallucinations, became disorientated in time and space, and lost their ability to think clearly, or to concentrate on anything for very long. Some of the symptoms lasted for a considerable time after they had been released.

This is only a single illustration of the evidence that *all* animals need to have their senses stimulated. And the need for stimulation also implies the need for *change*. The horse is always looking for something new – a horse that can see out and see things happening is far happier and far more alert than one that is gazing at a blank wall all day. He needs changing sounds, changing scenery, tastes and smells. Unlike the dog, the horse has in fact a somewhat limited sense of smell, but he still needs variation in the things he smells and tastes. The horse is naturally inquisitive and curious, and he needs to experience new things all the time.

Some years ago another American researcher corralled a group of wild mustangs, straight in off the Prairie, then drove each in turn singly into a smaller corral, in the middle of which was a blanket. Without exception each horse proceeded to walk round and round the blanket, in quite a short time to touch and smell it. Then, having done so, it ignores it – walking over it, dunging on it and taking no notice of it whatever.

Then in a further experiment, a slight change was made. Half of the subjects were left in the corral with the plain blanket, which they continued to ignore. The other half were herded into another corral where an inflatable bladder had been put under a blanket, which from time to time was inflated by remote control so that the centre of the blanket rose up in the air. When this happened the horses immediately retreated from the blanket, then began to investigate it again very cautiously. When this was continued for up to forty-eight hours these horses retained an interest in the moving blanket, where with the settled blanket they had come to ignore it within half an hour.

A horse is interested and intrigued by anything new. But he tends to get bored quickly once he has investigated an object and found that it is not dangerous or in any other way interesting. Only if it is moving, or appears different from time to time, will it retain his interest. We know from our own experience, both with stationary and moving objects, that single coloured objects will retain the horse's interest for less time than a multi-coloured or moving object. (That is not to say that a horse necessarily sees colours – even if he is colour blind, he will see different shades of grey, and varying shades are of greater interest than a plain grey). We also know that if an object makes a noise, it will be more interesting and of course more frightening, than an object which makes none.

Rostellan once gave us a good example of how a horse likes to change the pattern of noise around it. We had put up a block of five new loose boxes, and so that the horses could see out better we put in glass windows. The glass windows stayed intact for nearly a year. Then one day Rostellan accidentally broke a pane of glass. The noise of the glass falling on the concrete outside at first frightened him, then fascinated him. He put his head out through the window to see what had caused it. A piece of glass balancing on the edge fell to the ground with a tinkling noise, so he drew back and pushed out another. After that, whenever he was feeling a bit bored, he would use his nose to push out another piece of glass from the edge of the window, just to hear it shatter on the ground outside. Each time he pushed out a piece of glass, he would take half a step back and listen to the tinkle as it fell. Within four months he had managed to break every window on the place. He would break most of the glass at the first push, then proceed to push out all the fragments from the edge of the window one at a time, with his nose. After the first window we ceased to worry, since he never scratched or cut himself on the broken edge of the glass. And it didn't matter what I did to try and protect the windows: he somehow managed to break them every time. I even put wooden bars across them, and he caught hold of them one by one with his teeth, leant back and wrenched them off. After this I gave it up as a bad job, and just let him get on with it. Eventually I took out the windows, and blocked up the place where the windows had been, since I was not going to go on for ever putting in new panes of glass for Rostellan to break.

Just before this series of incidents, we had done a short trial with metal feed containers, but very quickly had to abandon it since the horses kept us awake all night with the noise the metal containers made all over the floor. I thought at first that the containers were being pushed round because there were stray bits of food on the edges or underneath and in the corners; or that they were being moved by chance. Then for a week I measured the distance that the metal containers had been shifted from their original spot in the corner, and this averaged out at just over five feet. This did not mean of course that the container had only been moved five feet in the night – from the row that was going on the horses seemed to be playing football with them. It only meant that in the morning the average distance of each container from where it had been left the previous night was five feet – it could have gone twenty times round the stable first for all we knew. We then changed the metal containers for plastic buckets, and discovered that though these were much easier and lighter to move than the metal ones, in the morning they were only a matter of a few inches from their original position. Since the feeding pattern in each case was exactly the same, and the food in the containers was exactly the same, we deduced that the heavy metal feed containers had been moved about to provide more noise stimulation for the horses.

We did make deliberate efforts to provide this stimulation. Because I thought they would enjoy it, I hung metal chains from their hay racks, so that they could entertain themselves during the night. But after forty-eight hours I had to take them out, because nobody could sleep for the ghostly clanking of chains. And since it was a question of depriving the horses of a plaything or the whole family of sleep, the horses lost their toys. But then I am a very hard, cruel and selfish man.

The conclusion to be drawn from all this, when you are training a horse, is that, if you can make what he is doing fun, and a game – in other words a source of constant excitement – the horse will enter into each new thing with a whole-hearted enthusiasm that at times is quite staggering.

If ever there was a horse who responded to excitement, it was Passing Cloud. He belonged to a friend of mine, Martin, who one hunt meeting managed to have a fall in an early race, and before he was carted off to hospital asked me to ride his grey in subsequent hunts, and school him a bit. He left me with the parting injunction not to do too much with him because he had only jumped a few hurdles and didn't know anything about point-to-point fences. So at the next race I lined up a bit behind the other horses at the start because I didn't want to get too involved with the field. But unfortunately I got a flier, and found myself leading into the first fence between two other horses. The young horse almost skidded to a halt trying to refuse, but we were going too fast so he shot straight up into the air as the best way out of his problem, and somehow or other we landed the other side, more or less together. And away we went again, with him really taking hold and enjoying himself. He was determined to catch up with everybody else, because the time it had taken us to negotiate the first fence had meant that we had fallen back from second or third place to last. This didn't deter him. He tore into the next fence, and since he had negotiated one obstacle by going straight up in the air, he went straight up in the air again, and again landed on the other side. By the time we had jumped the third fence he was beginning to get the hang of things and we didn't lose very much ground. I was quite happily keeping my place at the rear of the field, and so we completed the first circuit. By the time we passed the crowd for the first time, he had jumped seven or eight fences, and was taking off immaculately.

The first circuit had been very fast indeed, so as we went into the second, tired and beaten horses began to drop back past us. I didn't take any notice of these. I kept Passing Cloud going comfortably, and not pushing him. As we jumped the third last fence, however, I suddenly realized that I was lying in third place with a double handful under me. So I touched him with my heels, and the result was electric. He quickly caught up with the two leaders and met the second last fence absolutely perfectly. Between the second last and the last I passed the horse that was lying second. And went up to George Small who was riding a mare called Skittles. Both of us raced into the last fence, but Passing Cloud's inexperience was no match for Skittles' speed and jumping. He caught it an almighty clout, which almost brought him to a standstill, but we finished a comfortable second.

That was on Easter Sunday. And since Passing Cloud was none the worse for wear, Martin decided to run him again on Easter Monday, at the Taunton Vale, where we won the Maiden race by a distance.

The point is that to Passing Cloud at this stage of his career racing was a new and enjoyable game, so he put everything that he had into galloping and jumping. Whereas if he had been taught that galloping and racing was a chore, he would never have raced with the same success.

Of all the horse's sensory needs, perhaps the most striking to the observer is that for movement. Indeed a horse is almost *never* still. As the reader probably knows a horse never really goes to sleep: he merely dozes. And if you watch him at rest, you will see that he is constantly moving a leg, twitching an ear, moving his head slightly from side to side or up and down. First he will move one foot slightly, then put his weight on another one. When the horse is stabled, exactly the same thing happens. He spends most of the day and a large part of the night moving round the stable or shifting his muscles from time to time. If a door is open, he will stand looking out, but he will not be still: his head will be moving from side to side, and he will be moving his feet even when he is resting his body. He will be using and moving his muscles.

Now the point arises, is this movement simply a physical end in itself, or is there a psychological reason for it? As we saw earlier there was a psychological need for the horse to chew, and it seems more than probable that there is an equally in-built need for a horse's body to be moving at all times.

I had the opportunity to observe the extraordinary restlessness of a group of horses one morning last spring. Our cross-country course was in some need of repair after the bashing it had received during the previous winter, so choosing a nice sunny day I went up to carry out the necessary repairs.

In the field there was a herd of five horses: Rostellan, Bluebell,

Grayling, Flash and Madam. And when I got there they were all over in one corner. But as soon as I started work on the first of the fences, they drifted over to investigate, led by Rostellan. They stood watching me, no doubt to make sure that I didn't skimp my work. Rostellan then decided that I must have something to eat in my pocket, since it was bulging, so he started investigating with his prehensile lip and before I knew what he had done, he had my handkerchief between his teeth. The white flapping object was just the excuse he needed. He stood up on his hind legs, spun round, and galloped round in a circle shaking the thing.

Since he got no reaction from me – he was hoping that I would pursue him to get my handkerchief back – he went next to annoy Madam. Madam wasn't interested in off-white handkerchiefs, so she put back one ear and lazily waved a leg in his direction. Knowing what that meant, Rostellan decided to leave her alone. And since no one was interested in his game, he dropped my handkerchief and went over and started teasing Grayling. But Grayling wasn't interested in playing either and he was thirsty anyway, so he set off towards the stream to drink. The others came awake one by one, and in single file, with gaps of twenty to thirty yards between them, wandered slowly down to the water with him. Bluebell, once he had finished drinking, then took it into his head to strike the water with one fore-foot, and since this produced a nice splash, he did it again and again. Then he tried with the other one, and for the next five minutes proceeded to strike the water first with one foot and then with the other, soaking himself in the process, and everybody else, and making the water extremely muddy and unfit to drink.

Madam, who is not of a frivolous nature, drew her skirts about her like the angry Duchess she is, and stalked away from the coarse yobbos who were making all this splashing – the other horses having joined in the game with Bluebell – and with a reluctant look at the others, Flash, who was enjoying himself, followed his beloved Madam. And they wandered up from the stream, picking a bit of grass from here and there. Madam came across a nice bit of clover and started grazing seriously. Flash joined her. And the others drifted one by one up from the stream and started grazing too.

I had meanwhile finished repairing the second of the fences and felt that I had earned a rest. So I went and sat under the sunny side of the bank to smoke a cigarette. The horses saw me sitting down, and decided to come over and see what I was doing. After all it might have been their lucky day, and I could have been dead. First Flash and Madam came up and talked to me for a minute or two before going back to their grazing. Then Rostellan came up, quite sure that I was dangerous. He stopped five yards from me, put his nose out and sniffed. I didn't move. He took a couple of steps forward, and sniffed again. Still I didn't move. He came right up to me, and blew in my face. So I blew a mouthful of smoke back at him. And he drew back, thoroughly offended, which left the way open for Bluebell to come and chat. Bluebell is quite a favourite of mine – he's got a certain amount of character and an extremely nice temperament – so I managed to find him a couple of nuts, and this was too much for Rostellan, who came and shoved him to one side and demanded nuts as well. Which of course he got. Both of them then made a nuisance of themselves trying to persuade me to give them more, and since my restful cigarette had ceased to be restful I went back to mending my fences.

Without me to annoy, Rostellan and Bluebell had nothing to do but tease each other. Rostellan started nibbling Bluebell's front legs, and Bluebell retaliated by squealing and then taking a piece out of Rostellan's side. Rostellan swung his backside round at Bluebell and kicked vaguely in his direction. Bluebell shoved at Rostellan hitting him in the side with his shoulder. Rostellan pivoted on his hind legs, and for the next few minutes they both stood on their hind legs boxing each other. Then, tiring of their game of stallions, they decided to race, and half-way round one circuit of the field Grayling joined in. Then they were all extremely tired and went to sleep again, and they slept for the best part of an hour. But at no time did any of the four stay completely still.

One or another was always flicking an ear, moving a muscle. Rostellan was flapping his lips.

I had by then had the horses under reasonably close observation over a period of four hours, yet none of them had been completely still during that time even for a couple of minutes. There was no necessity for them to move at all, other than to graze or to go for water. Yet there was this need within them for constant movement.

When a mare is in season, Nature makes her even more restive, to satisfy her sexual need. In the wild this extra need to move about of course increased her chance of mating.

The fitter the horse is, too, the greater its need for movement. A horse that is over-fat, or in some way under-nourished, will move less, simply because Nature conserves what energy she can. But a fit, well horse needs movement all the time. No matter how long a horse has been domesticated, and how well bred it is, it still retains the impulses of the wild horse. And the fit wild horse that moved a lot had a much greater selection of grazing, and a much better balanced diet. This meant that by natural selection the horse that had the greatest need for activity and movement was most likely to survive. And the stallion that was constantly on the move was not only fitter and stronger, but was also more likely to sire a large number of foals than the lazy stallion who, like a Sultan in his harem, stayed in the same place waiting for the women to come to him. And in the same way the horse that even at rest was alert all the time, was far more likely to be able to escape a predator such as a wild dog, or wolf, than the horse who relaxed completely and slept deeply. So by natural selection, Nature ensured that those horses with the greatest need for activity and movement were those that survived and reproduced, and the horses which had very little drive for movement were the ones that didn't breed or died of starvation, or were eaten by other animals.

The constant movement of horses, on the other hand, rarely involves galloping about like cowboys chasing Indians. It usually means simply a slow walk, grazing and moving, and drinking.

In our observations of mountain ponies, we have seen them leave good grazing, just moving on, picking a bit here and a bit there, to quite poor grazing, and then staying there for an hour or two, then moving slowly back towards the good grazing. The urge to move from place to place is usually over a defined but quite large area – the natural grazing area of any herd of horses may be anything from two to five thousand acres – and they will naturally stay within that area, though of course they will change their grazing area according to the season. An active stallion on the other hand will cover an area grazed by four or five different herds.

This need for movement is not confined to horses: it applies to most animals. For example, even tame rats need to be constantly on the move. In some experimental work, tame rats were confined in a very small place, which restricted their movements, and then allowed to run on a wheel. It was discovered that the length of time the rat was confined in a small space was in direct relation to the length of time he ran in the wheel: in other words, a rat that had been confined for four hours ran twice as long as one that had been confined for two hours.

We have found this principle holds true in our own work with horses: a horse that is confined in a stable that restricts his movement to the absolute minimum for twelve hours, when released in a field, will canter round twice as long as the same horse when he is confined in a stable for only six hours.

8: *Social Behaviour – The Horse and the Herd*

All horses have a very great need for the company of other horses. This applies even to the loner, the horse that will almost always graze away from the other horses by himself. You may think from casual observations of him in the field that he has no need for the other horses, and yet if you move the main herd of horses from one field to another leaving him behind, he will try to follow, and if you leave him shut in the field by himself, he will soon be belting round, shouting to the others, 'Where the hell have you got to?'. He needs at least to be near a group of other horses.

And very closely linked with this need for company, is the need of some horses for real affection. Such a horse will make a particular friend of another horse, and the two will become inseparable. If you move his particular friend from the herd, that horse will be as upset as if you had moved the whole herd away. If on the other hand you move the herd leaving the pair behind, they will both try and follow the main body of the herd.

This of course is one of the first of the natural habits that has to be modified when you are training a horse, since a horse is no use at all if he won't go away from other horses. And a close friendship link, though it may be used in the education of a young or difficult horse, may well be a nuisance if it prevents him from doing anything by himself. We had an example of such a close friendship between Flash and Madam, both of whom were sent to us for gentling two years ago.

Madam, as the reader will remember, is a bad-tempered mare whom not everyone has cause to love. But, in spite of her awkwardness, Flash adored her. And where Madam went, Flash went too. Flash, being part Arab, wasn't a natural jumper, but

Madam was, and since Flash wanted to stay near Madam he had to jump to keep up with her. And he turned into a superb jumper, and an extremely good cross-country horse.

The summer of 1974 was extremely wet and cold, and Flash with the Arab strain in him began to lose condition, so we decided to keep him in all the time. Madam, being of much hardier New Forest stock, was thriving under the same conditions, so we kept on turning her out at night. But we very quickly had to turn Flash out again too. He totally and absolutely refused to eat in the stable, unless Madam was there as well. We tried feeding him when she was there, but he was still not getting enough food in him to last him through the twenty-four hours – especially since the rest of the time he was pacing in his box screaming his head off, and wasn't relaxing and sleeping at all.

The closest ties between horses are usually between mare and gelding, particularly between a strong-charactered mare and a rather weak-charactered gelding: rather in the same way as among human beings you may find an exceptional bond between a very big strong-charactered woman and a weak rather insignificant little man.

This need for affection has its roots in an old response to fear. When a foal is frightened, it will return to its mother for affection and protection, and only once it has received the expected signs of affection from its mother will it begin to show its curiosity again. If something frightens a foal, it will gallop back to its mother, who will nuzzle it and say 'It's quite safe, mother is here'. Then when the foal has been reassured, it will go first to look at, and then to investigate, the object that alarmed it.

This need for reassurance/affection is hard to test in laboratory conditions with horses, because the foal is rather a large and difficult animal for laboratory conditions. But an animal that has been tested in this way is the monkey. Within two to ten days of birth a baby monkey moves round on its own, and manipulates objects, so scientists can measure what it does and does not do, and what it responds to. It can suckle a bottle and be reared in artificial conditions which can be chosen at will.

Monkeys were used in an interesting series of experiments on affection, in one of which monkeys were raised singly in cages providing a comfortable environment and adequate care of their bodily needs. In each cage two artificial mothers were put: one was a wire mesh cylinder with a block of wood where the head would be – this was called the wire mother; the other was an artificial mother made from sponge rubber, and sheath towelling – this was called the cloth mother. Behind each mother was put a light bulb which provided radiant heat for the baby monkey, and either mother could be fitted with a bottle where her breast would be. The purpose of the experiment was to see how much time the infant monkey spent with each mother, when that mother had the bottle.

The experiment was designed to test the theory that love was learned through rewarding the baby monkey's hunger motive, and the results showed that the monkeys strongly preferred the cloth mother, regardless of where the bottle was. They spent fifteen hours more per day with the cloth mother than with the wire mother, even though not more than one hour was spent feeding. At twenty-one to twenty-five days, when the wire mother had the bottle, the baby monkeys still spent at least eighteen hours with the cloth mother and when the cloth mother had the bottle they spent twenty-three hours a day with the cloth mother, and only one with the wire mother.

Two conclusions can be drawn from this experiment: first that the monkey has an unlearned tendency to be near mother; and second that this tendency was one of seeking contact and reassurance from the mother – that is, it was not exclusively related to the taking of food.

The only work of this nature that has been done with foals was with artificially reared thoroughbreds who were fed by an automatic feeder near, or at a distance from, a source of heat, i.e., a heating lamp. The foals did considerably better, up to fifteen percent in body weight at five months, when the artificial feeder was near the heat lamp, than when it was at some distance from it: the most important factor was found to be the heat.

Also, the foals spent at least two hours a day more near the heat lamp when it was against straw bales than when it was placed next to a wooden partition, or a stone wall: the best result was obtained with a block of bales two feet long and three feet high, next to the artificial feeder with the heat at the end nearest the feeder. In these conditions, the foals fed more readily and easily, and made considerably more body weight, and it was thought – though no methodical observation was taken – that they were taking more exercise and were more venturesome than the foals that had to walk from the heat lamp to the feeder.

Emotional and temperamental qualities will of course vary from horse to horse even more than directly physical ones. The need for movement, for example, is very slight in some horses, who will be quite happy to stand around flicking an ear, or moving from leg to leg and doing absolutely nothing else, while other horses will spend the whole day walking round and round in their box. This need for movement in some horses is so great that they need hardly be *exercised* at all – they keep themselves fit wherever they are.

Old Cork Beg, for example, was never still in his loose box. He would stand at the door looking out for a couple of minutes, then walk to the back of the box and take a mouthful of hay, or a sip of water, or just walk round the box, then go back and look out of the door again. He did this so much that it was extremely difficult to get any condition on him. But once you got him fit, he needed very little exercise.

At the other extreme is Royalty, who will stand in one corner of her box all day, positioned so that she can look out through the door and if she feels like it take a mouthful of hay, just moving from one foot to another – with her head slightly to one side so that she can see out better. There is hardly any other movement at all. This makes her an easy horse to have in the stable, because there is only one corner of the box to clean out. But she has to be exercised regularly, to prevent her from becoming sluggish and fat.

The same variation is to be found in the degree of curiosity exhibited by one horse and another. Some horses are very curious and some horses couldn't care less. Equally, when it comes to competitiveness, some horses are good competitors, and others don't mind whether they are beaten or not.

In fact many of these motives seem to be linked together in a type of horse personality: the lively active horse tends to be the one that is also curious and a good competitor. The lazy sleepy horse is much less likely to be curious, and if he is very lazy he can't be bothered to compete. These are examples of what might be termed linked motives. Greed and laziness too go together; and high sexuality in a mare tends to be linked with irritableness. It is worthwhile remembering that very often these needs and motives can be linked together, and that certain motives may be linked with certain vices.

For example, a very sociable horse will tend to be nappy. Laziness in a horse will also mean that he tends to refuse a jump if he can, and laziness of course, like everything, is a motive. The reason for the horse's laziness is the negative desire to do anything. Motives of course can be negative, as well as positive. The desire to be with other horses can be termed what we call a social motive. Social motives are the reasons for the horse's behaviour with other horses, and of course with his owner and rider. Some of these will be learned and others are born in the horse, and even those that are born within the horse can be modified by his handling, and what he has learned.

Because of their size and habits, there has been very little laboratory research into these motives in horses. Most of it has been carried out on animals that fit into the hygienic white-coated environment of the laboratory better – such as human beings, monkeys, rats and dogs. But most of this research can be applied to the horse and has been verified by our observations of the horse.

The supreme competitor was Molfre. Molfre at home is an absolutely superb jumper, and will place himself at a jump and jump four foot of fixed timber with no difficulty at all. It is obvious when you are riding him that he enjoys the challenge of jumping timber, and he also enjoys placing himself correctly at a fence and jumping it perfectly. He will give a little flick of his tail each time he has cleared a fence. If he makes a very slight mistake, his annoyance is obvious. But when he is racing, it is a different cup of tea altogether. The excitement of the race and his competitive urge completely override his desire to jump perfectly and he is a very chancey fencer indeed. He will jump most of the fences superbly but if he is wrong, it's a question of just bash on regardless, and hope for the best. At times Molfre and I land up on the ground and, at other times, we end up with me clasping him in a loving embrace around his neck, desperately trying to find out where the hell my saddle has got to.

I rode Molfre in the Players Gold Leaf Point-to-Point Championship qualifier at Ludlow in 1974. The field went off like bats out of hell and I managed to drop him in at the back of the field. Without very much difficulty we completed the first circuit more or less in the rear of the field, and he jumped every fence absolutely superbly, meeting it right, placing himself, and gaining lengths on each jump. At the beginning of the second circuit, I started moving up through the field, mainly because the other horses were tiring fast, and partly because of Molfre's fantastic jumping. He was standing right back and rocketing over the fences, and gaining lengths each time. There was a fairish run from the fourth last to the third last fence, and by the time we had jumped the fourth last fence, I had moved up to sixth place. When we got to the third last, I moved up into fourth place, going infinitely better than any of the other horses. I was sitting on a double handful and was beginning to wonder by how many lengths I would win. I could see Knightsbridge, who was just in front of me, rolling from side to side with fatigue, and the two other horses in front of him were also tiring rapidly. But my luck was out. Knightsbridge, who was just in front of me, fell and this distracted Molfre's attention at the crucial moment. He took off a stride too far back and we hit the fence going fast, and we both slid twenty yards the other side. His sheer competitive nature when he came to racing and jumping had overridden his desire to jump properly, and the result was that we ended flat on our faces in the mud!

One of the first things we notice about our horses is their very great need for the company of other horses. This can be observed in foals from the very beginning. The foal at first will stay entirely by its mother's side. Over the course of the next three or four months, it will start venturing away a few steps at a time. Then it will meet and play with other foals. And at approximately a year old in its natural state, it will leave its mother entirely and choose other companions for which it shows a great affection. Horses don't like being by themselves. And though this desire for company may be stronger in some horses than others, the herding instinct always survives.

This need for companionship reflects a number of separate but closely linked needs. One is the need to give and receive affection – which it expresses with its owner, its close companions or its offspring. A second is its more general need to be with other horses, be they friendly or not; this is an inherited need, with its roots in the wild when the chances of survival were considerably greater for a horse in a large herd than for one grazing by himself. In times of stress horses will always group together in a bunch, receiving bodily contact and reassurance from other members of the group. And a third, and related, need is the horse's urge to know his own particular place in the hierarchy of the herd.

It is the ancient herding instinct that makes a horse that loses his rider head for the nearest group of horses. I've seen a horse travel three miles to get to a herd when he was turned loose on the mountain. The nearest group of horses in sight was on the other side of the valley, which was nearly three miles away, so as soon as he was set free, he stood for a few moments looking round, saw the group of horses on the skyline, called to them, and proceeded to take the shortest and most direct route to reach them. When he finally got there, the herd leader came out and kicked his teeth in for intruding within the group. The strange horse stayed on the fringes of the group for two or three days before he was absorbed and accepted by the group.

One of the mysterious things about this need to join the herd is that the horse always seems compelled to take the most direct route, even if it means surmounting quite difficult obstacles in order to do so. We saw this peculiarity in Jezebel when we wanted to keep her in for the stallion. When we turned the horses out that night, instead of letting Jezebel loose with them, we left her shut in her loose box, but as soon as she realized that the other horses were going out without her, she jumped the three-foot-six lower half of her door, on to the concrete. And then, instead of turning right to go down to the front gate as she did three times a day at least, she jumped the railing in front of the stables – which again stands at three-foot-six high – crossed to the other side of the railings, dropped another six feet from the bank on to the drive to the house, then over a two-foot-six wire fence which drops away a further six feet to the road below. The further the horses went away from her, the stronger seemed her need to join them. But it would still have been just as quick and considerably easier for her to have trotted down to the front gate than to take those three very difficult jumps, fantastic jumper though she is. She seemed compelled to go in a straight line. I have also seen a horse that normally wouldn't take off from the ground if an atom bomb was set off under its backside jumping sheep netting with barbed wire on top to get to a strange group of horses, when he had been turned out by himself. Then when the rest of his own herd were turned out after him, he jumped the fence the other way to get back.

A bunch of four unbroken Welsh Cobs we once kept had the run of three fields. They were accustomed to going from one field to another through the opened gateways. But one day, for some reason, Phoenix got left behind when his companions moved on to the adjoining field. All he had to do to join them was to go down to the gateway. Yet what he did was to canter up to the wire fence, and jump it. Like Jezebel, he took the more difficult but direct, route in order to reach the herd.

This very deep inherent need to be with its companions can be used very effectively when breaking and gentling a horse. The thing to do is to work him together with a group of other, broken, horses. First he will try to behave as the big boys are behaving, which will make him better behaved; and second, he will receive reassurance from the group, and so will go much more happily. Riding a young horse, after all, is making him do something that is strange and repugnant to him, at the same time as trying to break a behaviour pattern which has been his for the previous three or four years, so the presence of other horses can be very reassuring – though it also has its risks.

At one time we were breaking large groups of horses together, and riding them together, and this worked extremely well. Most of the time they all behaved perfectly – you could see them competing to show how well they could perform. But just occasionally one of them would explode. And then they would all explode, one after another, like a series of fire crackers, and you would have people falling off, and bodies scattered all over the mountain.

My father used to have an extremely good method of teaching foals to accept a halter. He used to put a halter on to a foal, then tie the halter rope to its mother's tail. The foal, when it felt the strangeness and the strain of the halter, would fight a little bit. But then he would automatically go to his mother for reassurance, which meant that the rope went slack. This would go on for ten minutes to a quarter of an hour. Compared with the normal method of tying the foal up and leaving him to fight it out, this was a remarkably quick and peaceful way of accustoming the foal to a halter. The foal was taught to lead in exactly the same way. With the foal still tied to her tail, the mare would lead and as soon as the foal saw its mother going away, he would try to follow her. So he very quickly learned that the tug from the halter meant that he had to go forward.

A similar method was also used by the Mohawk Indians when

they were training a horse. When a horse was to be backed, he would be tied extremely tightly to an old horse for a day or two, and led round with his head on the old horse's shoulder. When he was used to this, and going quite happily, a rider would get on him. This method made it impossible for the horse to buck, since he couldn't get his head down. And since he was already accustomed to walking beside the old horse, he very quickly learned to go quietly when he was ridden.

Both these methods illustrate how what can very often be a frightening experience to a young horse, and an awkward time for his handler, can be made simple and easy by using one horse's natural desire to be near another.

Within the herd the horse also needs an assured place within the seniority pattern of the herd. And the place he finds is a fair indication of his temperament and ability. The dominant, the independent, the bloody-minded and bad-tempered will be at the top of the social structure; while the lazy and weak-charactered will be at the bottom. But each horse within the group needs the approval and acceptance of the group as a whole. And this need for approval applies equally to horses which are being handled by man. The horse will perform quite exceptionally for the person for whom he has special respect and affection. And both of these are needed: affection without respect is useless, just as respect without affection will severely limit the amount the horse will do for its rider. Yet within the herd the need for respect does not have anything to do with the need to be liked – it is quite simply a need to have an established and recognized position in society.

In our own herd, at the top of the social scale are Madam and Jack. Madam is very much a loner, and except by Flash, who dogs her heels and adores her, she is liked by none of the other horses. When I go into the field with a bucket of nuts to feed them, she'll attack and kick anything who approaches me, other than Flash. When the horses are driven in from the field, Madam will refuse to allow anything else to pass her, either by driving at the other horse backwards with her teeth, or by kicking as it comes up to her. So she may be liked by none of the other horses, but they do respect her. She's got an established position as the herd boss, and woe betide anything that threatens her authority. Jack has an equal position with Madam at the top of the herd, a situation they are able to maintain because they tend to avoid each other so that they don't clash. When I go into the field with the bucket of nuts, Jack will approach from the opposite side to Madam, so that I am between them, and there can be no conflict. When they are coming in from the field, Jack does not contest Madam's place at the head. He will punch anyone who infringes his dignity, but he doesn't hammer anything unless it is misbehaving. He is a very sociable animal, is well liked by the herd and will always be found in the middle of the group.

Flash being under Madam's protection neither is hammered, nor hammers, since he is a very sweet kind horse. And he has his own secure position within the herd. Jezebel and Biddy, being my special horses, and Rostellan, being my wife's horse, have each a very strong social position within the herd, because they are under our protection for a lot of the time. When they are out in the field the other horses will tend to leave them alone, and provided they don't invade their special preserves, neither Madam nor Jack will bother them.

At the bottom end of the social scale come Swallow, Grayling, Zoom and Gypo, who tend to stick to a group by themselves, and keep away from the herd bosses because they are automatically hammered. But at the same time, should any strange horse intrude, that is a new horse be turned out with them, they would be protected by the strength of the herd bosses, so they feel safe within the group.

The social acceptance necessary for each horse within a herd is, as I have said, very similar to the approval the horse needs from its rider, or the person who is handling it. And when a horse goes to a new owner a battle ensues very like the battle that takes place within the horse herd to decide who is boss, and whether the new member is going to be in the top, the middle, or the bottom end of the social spectrum. And your horse is likely to relate to you in a way not unlike the way he relates to other horses.

If you get a horse that has been at the bottom end of the herd, he will be comparatively easy to handle, at least to begin with, because he is accustomed to being bossed around by other horses, and will accept the authority of a new owner quite readily. If, on the other hand, you get a horse who has a dominant personality, and has thus been accustomed to being the boss of the herd, he will try and dominate his new owner. He will be probing for weak spots in his rider, testing whether his owner has a strong or a weak personality, whether he is a good horseman or a bad one. And he will very quickly make use of any weakness. At this stage it is extremely important to be firm but kind with a new horse, and to punish any infringement of discipline instantly – and punishment is not necessarily, of course, flaying the skin off his backside with a hunting crop. It can be a quiet 'stop it', or if the horse persists, a slap on the nose, or the nearest offending portion, is usually enough. What is necessary is to establish yourself as herd boss, *not* the horse.

However, in addition to the security of being a member of a group, it is also essential for a horse's wellbeing to be able to think well of itself. (This is relevant to its position within the herd too, because the horse that thinks well of itself will naturally be high in the social hierarchy). And if he has a high opinion of his own abilities, he will constantly strive to do his best, while other horses who have a low opinon of themselves will do only the minimum to avoid punishment. This need for some horses to assert themselves regardless of what the rest of the herd may think, this need for self-esteem, is shown in a variety of ways. The horse, in asserting itself over other horses to obtain power within the herd, may need to beat the other horses when it is galloping with them, or to jump fences better than the other horses. So this ambition can be channelled to get the horse to succeed in competition: in fact we go to great lengths to build up a horse's self-esteem when we want it to compete.

For example, when I am training my horses for point-to-pointing or hunter-chasing, I make quite sure that I don't gallop them with horses that they cannot beat quite easily. I want them to get used to winning, so that their self-esteem will be built up, and at the same time they will feel an increasing need to win.

If, over a period, one observes horses in competitive work – showjumping, eventing or racing for example – it is difficult to avoid the conclusion that there is a natural drive within some horses to do something well, simply to achieve a competence for its own sake alone. Some horses have this need to excel, to do something better than any other horse. Even when they are not competing such horses have this need to be supreme. This need must not be confused with the need to compete – for the same thing can be seen in a super beginner's pony who takes terrific pride in taking care of his young rider well.

Jack is an example of what I mean. He is an extremely good and very fast pony, and at times he takes great pleasure in depositing a rider who gets too presumptuous firmly on the ground. But when he has a very nervous person or a complete beginner on his back, he will take great pride in looking after him, and giving him as much confidence as possible. You will see him pacing forward with his ears pricked and his neck arched, putting one foot carefully in front of another, making sure that his young rider is absolutely secure. There is nothing competitive about this: it is purely Jack's desire to do whatever he is doing as well as he possibly can.

Not all horses have this quality – there are others who seem to take a perverse pride in doing as little as possible without punishment. But many have, and in training it is invaluable.

This urge to excel again is something that has come down from the primitive horse, since the horse that was the biggest, strongest, fastest, and most mentally dominant was the one that had the best grazing, and was the best able to escape from any predators. He was also the one, if he was a stallion, who had the greatest number of mares, and sired most of the next generation of foals. Similarly a mare who was mentally dominant, and physically the strongest, and fastest, was much more likely to live through the rigours of the winter than her weaker-willed sisters.

If you remove pride from a horse, you will remove his will to win and his will to succeed. This is why a horse that has been broken and cowed will never be so good a horse as one who has been allowed to develop slowly and naturally.

You can destroy a horse's pride by allowing him repeatedly to be beaten in a race. Or you can equally do so by over-racing him. For example, if your horse is successfully jumping three-foot, and jumping spreads of three-foot-six or four-foot, you can build up his pride and his self-confidence, so that if you face him at a four-foot fence with a five-foot spread, he will indeed attempt to jump it. But if he fails, and fails the next time he tries to jump a big fence, you will completely have destroyed his pride and his self-confidence so that even when you put him back to the three-foot fences he will refuse to jump them. Self-esteem is a very fragile thing and you will have to go back to fences two-foot and two-foot-six high, that he can step over, to build up his pride again over a considerable period of time. Pride and self-esteem can only be built with patience, and gradually, and no horse should be pushed too far too fast. Even the toughest and most obstinate horse is vulnerable.

We once had a very dominant yearling. He was a rather unpleasant horse, and a terrific bully, who hunted and chivvied the other young horses relentlessly. So to cure him of this we put him in with three or four very strong, tough horses. And for the next week or so, they hammered the living daylights out of him. Then we put him back with his companions, whom he had previously been bullying to distraction, and instead of being the boss of the herd, he was right at the bottom end of it. His pride had been shattered, and for a considerable time until he had built up some self-respect again, the youngsters that he had previously bullied, were bullying him.

A horse however has an inbuilt need to be aggressive. This is part of his survival equipment. Without this aggression, he would always be driven away from the best grazing, be the last one to get water, and at the back of the line the one most exposed to danger. But how much the aggression is innate and how much learned, it is very difficult to say: as always, it is hard to separate genetically inherited characteristics from those conditioned by environment and by training.

Early environment is extremely important. The size and strength of the foal when he first meets other foals will, for instance, condition his future attitude to other horses: if the other foals are bigger and stronger than him, he will tend to be bullied, and subservient; whereas if he is bigger and stronger than they, he will boss them. And if he is big and strong when he is weaned from his mother in the autumn, his ability to convert food will be good, he will winter well, and be stronger and more robust than his companions in the spring. So his early environment will play a considerable part in deciding how he copes with the hurly burly of herd life.

Then the inherited characters will come into play. At times the boss of the herd will not be the biggest, strongest foal or yearling. He may be a very aggressive smaller foal, bred from dominant parents.

On the other hand, training in aggression will start from the time he is born. If he is accustomed to his mother bossing the other horses, he will imitate her in his behaviour towards the other foals, but if his mother is in a subordinate position in the herd the foal will be trained by its mother to move away from the herd bosses when confronted by them.

Early handling by the human species is influential too. If from its earliest weeks the foal is allowed to misbehave, and get its own way, it will be extremely difficult to handle later on. It will lack respect for human beings, and consequently also affection, since an animal tends to be less affectionate towards those whom it doesn't respect. It is thus important to dominate a foal, that is make it do what it is told, from the beginning, so that when you come to handle and ride it, it will be disposed to co-operate.

When we are talking about boss horses, of course, we are really talking only about some ten percent of the herd: that is, in a group of ten horses one will probably be very strong-charactered; one very weak-charactered, bullied by everything else; a couple more may be fairly strong-charactered or weak-charactered, but the sixty or seventy percent of the horses in the middle of the herd will tend to be easy-going and easily handled. It is the ten percent strong-charactered horses, however, that I am interested in, since they provide the greatest challenge to the rider, and the greatest reward – for they are the ones with the strength of character to make use of every ounce of their ability.

9: *Emotion In Horses*

Emotion is a very powerful force in the behaviour of a horse. Fear, anger and excitement can all make a horse act in a way quite different from his normal pattern.

But what is emotion? It means several things. One of them is a physical state: a change in the chemical balance in the body, or in muscular tension; and another is the feeling arising out of the physical state. This feeling may be pleasant or unpleasant, but it cannot be seen or heard. It can be recognized only by the signs and sounds that the horse makes. You can see if a horse is frightened, if he is angry or if he is excited by the way he behaves. And you also can see their opposites – all emotions including fear, anger and excitement, have their opposites. As we want to avoid strong emotion in horses, it is the opposite states we are seeking: confidence, co-operation, calm. Thus it is important to understand what causes emotional changes, particularly extreme changes, so that the causes can be avoided.

A horse may do something because he is excited, or he may do something to become excited, because a horse enjoys excitement. The very sight of a jump may send some horses into a tizzy of excitement; and other horses are made excited by jumping. So a horse may jump because he is excited. Or he may jump to become excited. And he easily gets into a state where the more he feeds his excitement, the more excited he becomes. In a similar way, if you are shoeing a horse he may get angry because you are picking up, pulling about, and banging his feet. He kicks because he is angry, and the more he kicks, the angrier he becomes.

What happens is that any kind of emotion, anger, fear or excitement, arouses the horse. Intense emotion is a state of being highly aroused. And when the horse is highly aroused, he is more

144

likely to react to situations with strong emotion, so a spiral of intensifying emotion quickly develops which can get beyond your or his control. If a horse becomes excited at the thought of jumping fences, he will be even more excited after he has jumped the fence. So he will tear into the next one, more than likely making a complete mess of it and go flat on his face. The more excited a horse becomes, the more likely he is to make mistakes. In the same way, if you clobber a nervous horse he will become more frightened of you and all future attempts to catch him will make him even more frightened.

Emotion thus feeds upon emotion. The only cure is quietness on your part. If you are relaxed you can make the horse relax. Or you can put him with another horse who is relaxed and quiet, and this will steady him down. When a horse becomes aroused emotionally the muscles of his body tighten, his adrenal glands work overtime, his rate of breathing tends to increase, and his heart speeds up slightly. And though, when we are competing, we want the old adrenalin pumping, we don't want too much of it.

In competition of course a certain amount of excitement is inevitable. The difficulty is in keeping the level under control. The level of arousal that is required to stimulate an emotional response varies from horse to horse, depending on how the horse is bred, and how he has been handled. And the difference in temperament between one horse and another may be considerable.

If you set off a bomb behind a horse like Pudding, he would stay relaxed. I've seen Pudding grazing in a field, and two low-flying aircraft go past within fifty feet of him, one of which broke the sound barrier just as it passed him. And Pudding didn't even lift his head to look at them. Admittedly we are in an air force training area, and he is reasonably accustomed to low-flying aircraft. But so am I, and on this particular occasion they made me jump out of my skin. But Pudding just went on grazing as if nothing had happened. Pudding is a very placid horse. Nothing ever excites him, fusses him, frightens him, or makes him angry. He just goes on in his own quiet, sweet way.

At the other extreme is Royalty who had been mishandled in an attempt to break her as a three-year-old, as I shall later describe. When I got her, she wasn't particularly difficult to gentle, but she remained very nervous, and anything strange upsets her. She needs a lot of sympathy and understanding.

When we first had her the rustle of a paper bag in the next stable would send her into a near panic. On one occasion, shortly after she arrived, instead of carrying her feed in to her in the bucket I left it in the paper feed bag and emptied it from the feed bag into the bucket. And of course to get all the food out of the feed bag, I had to shake the bag. I did this unthinkingly. The next thing I knew, Royalty was climbing up the wall in a state of sheer frenzy, and it took me nearly an hour to get her to settle down and eat her feed. I couldn't of course allow Royalty to get into a state every time anyone rustled a paper bag, so I got her over it quite simply, once I got her settled down. I shook the paper feed bag gently, but nearer and nearer her until she took no notice of it. But still anything strange or unexpected sends her into a near panic. She is a horse, as we all recognize, with a very low arousal point indeed.

I have been hunting hounds off her this winter. The first time I got her hunting with the hounds, they worried her considerably. And if I berated the hounds, or waved my hunting crop, she became very upset indeed. But after four or five days she accepted the hounds, and even the hunting crop, though I still had only to curse the hounds to get her nervous again. She couldn't understand that I was not swearing at her – she thought that whatever it was was her fault. But eventually she settled down completely, and became one of the best hunters I have ever ridden.

These are two extremes of course. But even horses that have been brought up together, and handled by the same people all their lives, will vary in their emotional level. One may have two horses in neighbouring loose boxes, one of which will sleep all day and the other spend the whole day wandering round and round his box in a mild state of excitement, all the time alert to anything that is happening outside. The point at which he becomes aroused is simply much lower than that of his companion, so he will need to walk around more. He will eat less, he will dance about all over the road when you are riding him, and he will be a much better jumper than his companion whose one ambition is to stand still and go to sleep, and a much better race horse. The adrenalin in his blood will be pumping so fast that he just has to tear into the fence, and jump it, he just has to reach that winning post first. The size of his adrenal glands will be large, and his muscular development will be completely different from that of his sleepy friend because he has used his muscles in a completely different way.

One emotion can also change very easily into another: fear can change to excitement, and excitement to anger at the drop of a hat.

About four years ago I had a very excitable horse, a big sixteen-two thoroughbred called Sally Boy. We used to call him Boyo, and he really was a Boyo. He was an infuriating horse to exercise because he never walked in a straight line, he would dance from one side of the road to another, and since I had to work him for an hour-and-a-half to two hours a day, I found him very tiring. One day I had had enough, so I decided for the last half mile home I would make him walk every step. Every time he came out of a walk, I would stop, back him a stride, and then make him walk forward again. On an average, for every two strides he walked, he was going back one. And it took me two-and-a-half hours to cover that last half mile. In actual fact I never quite got him there. After about five hundred yards his excitement had changed to anger and he was in a tearing rage. We had been having a battle on the same spot for a solid ten minutes, when he finally went up on his hind legs and came back on top of me on the bank. I managed to stay in the saddle, and he scrambled to his feet. But I had lost my stirrups and my reins, and before I could retrieve them we were going back up the mountain flat out, with Boyo in complete charge. Three miles further on I managed to stop him, having weaved past four or five cars, petrifying the drivers and nearly killing myself and Boyo.

I stopped him by turning him straight into a solid wall of young fir trees, which he crashed into. But they made him lose his balance and he came down. Always making the most of my opportunities, I very quickly sat on his head, got out my cigarettes and matches and proceeded to have a smoke, while he simmered down, and I simmered down. After my second cigarette I let him get up. A two-and-a-half-hour battle and a three-mile gallop to end up with had taken most of the fizz out of Boyo, so when I got on him and set him off for home, he walked, he didn't jog. Two or three times he started dancing, and I turned him round and made him walk away until he had settled down again. And eventually, very, very late for my dinner, which I had to eat in the doghouse, we got home in one piece with a few scratches but otherwise no damage done.

Fear, as I have said, can be mixed with pleasure. And so can anger. Some horses positively enjoy being slightly frightened. If there is nothing startling in the hedge, and they are feeling a bit bored, they will imagine things to shy at and frighten themselves. Others will get great pleasure from the surge of anger they get out of a battle with their rider. In fact, fear, pleasure and anger can all be mixed together.

The overall aim of all our work might be said to be to give the horses pleasure. This is not a piece of altruism: it is very practical. If your aim is to give your horse pleasure, your horse is going to enjoy what he is doing, and if he is enjoying what he is doing he will put everything he has got into it. And you are bound to enjoy yourself more. This is what all horse psychology is about. It is about finding the easiest way to make a horse *want* to do something. There are many things that give a horse pleasure. A horse will get pleasure when he has done what he has wanted to do, and he will get pleasure from eating his dinner. This is a fact we know, so we make use of it. We put a little bit of his dinner in our pockets, for instance, and when he has done something well, we give him a tit-bit.

Similarly, we know a horse enjoys affection. So we give him plenty of affection and make a great fuss of him when he jumps or does something else well for us. Then he will not only get pleasure from jumping the fences, he will also get pleasure because you are pleased with him. And he will probably get more pleasure from the admiration and applause of the crowd. And one pleasure will reinforce another, all combining to make him excel in performance.

Biddy, for example, loves jumping cross-country fences. She will show her pleasure by the way she tears into the fences. But even if someone else is riding her, she will come back to me for praise when she has completed her round. And if I don't give her any she will nudge with her nose to remind me that I have not told her what a clever girl she is.

The things that give a horse pleasure will change with his training and his development. If you put your hand on an untouched foal of two or three weeks, he will be so badly frightened that he will run back to his mother in sheer terror. But the same foal, a month or two later, after he has known you and been handled by you, will come to be touched and stroked, and will show his pleasure. Similarly, an untouched horse off the mountain, if you put him into a loose box with a bucket of corn, will be terrified by the bucket and the corn. But a week or so later, when he has discovered what corn is, and that the bucket won't hurt him, will be bellowing 'where is my bloody breakfast?' when you appear with the bucket.

So with training – and everything you do with a horse is training – a horse's idea of what is pleasant will change considerably. In the case of the foal, fear has been transformed by affection. To start with, you were strange to the foal, and when you touched him he was frightened and ran back to his mother for reassurance. But when he got to know you, the touch of your hand did not arouse fear, so much as curiosity.

Fear on the other hand can be induced by training. I was called out last summer to a farm near Lampeter, to deal with a foal who was completely unmanageable and terrified. She had been teased by a horde of small boys from the neighbourhood, who had made great sport of chasing and running after her. By the time I was sent for the creature was so completely terrified of human beings that no one could get near her, or touch her, she was in such a state of terror. The foal was a registered cob filly, but the owner had decided he would have to sell her because he could not do anything with her.

I quickly realized what had caused the original trouble, but the problem now was how to undo the damage. With a lot of time and patience we eventually got the mare and foal out of the field and into the farm yard. Using an old pony, Topsy, as 'schoolmaster', we managed to get the mare and foal into a loose box and from then on it was all plain sailing. We just left the old pony in with the mare and foal for a couple of hours. Then I went back in. The foal tried to climb the walls of the loose box in absolute terror. But I kept old Topsy between me and her all the time, so that the foal began to feel that I wasn't threatening her in any way. After a minute or two, she stopped by her mother's side. I pushed Topsy until she went over by the foal, then I got the tips of my fingers on the foal, very, very gently. She shot round, but after four or five attempts, when I touched the foal again, she shook with terror but didn't move away. Then very, very gently I worked my hand all over her body. Old Topsy got bored about half way through and went from underneath my arm, so that I was standing right next to the foal. But by this time she was beginning to realize that I wasn't going to hurt her, and stood still, and after four or five sessions like this she began to look forward to seeing me, and settled down quite happily.

This is an example of how early experiences can first arouse fear of an object, in this case the human being, and then dispel that fear.

The difference between fear and anxiety is important, especially when we start to study the personality of a horse. Fear is aroused when the horse can recognize what causes that fear, and know what it is afraid of. Anxiety on the other hand is a vague fear that a horse will experience without knowing what causes it: a horse can be made uneasy and anxious by the memory of something that happened a long time ago, or by an alteration in the routine or pattern of his life.

I had an example of this distinction last summer. During the summer the pack of hounds I hunt are kennelled at the knacker's yard. This is for convenience, since the food supply there is on the spot. During the early part of the cub-hunting season we hunt hounds from there, in the surrounding area, so that any hounds that are missing can find their way back without any difficulty. It happened that I had borrowed a pony to ride cub-hunting, and the first day I rode up to the knacker's yard, the pony flatly refused to enter it. There was no apparent reason for this: there was a slightly unpleasant smell, but not a strong one, and it wasn't the noise that the hounds were making that was frightening, since the pony had already been hunted for two seasons. But it simply and flatly refused to go in. When I tried to make it do so, it shook with fear. Now I could have overcome this fear with a bit of a battle, but there was very little point in doing so, so I simply left the pony outside the yard while I got the hounds out, and we went off and had quite a pleasant day's hunting.

Then towards the end of the day, one of the perennial curses of this area, a low-flying aircraft, came over the trees and thoroughly frightened the pony. It carted me for about a hundred yards before I could stop it and quieten it.

These two incidents clearly demonstrate the difference between anxiety and fear: the first case, when there was no apparent reason for the pony's state of nerves, was anxiety. The second, when the source of the fear was easily identifiable – that is, the low-flying aeroplane – was fear.

Anxiety too can be induced. A classic experiment might be simultaneously to blow a whistle and hit a horse, or administer a mild electric shock, and to do that over a period of two or three weeks, four or five times a day. Two, three or even four years later you would produce anxiety in the horse simply by blowing the whistle. Needless to say we have not carried out this experiment ourselves, but it has been carried out on dogs, and the dogs retained the memory of an unpleasant experience associated with the whistle after a period of four years. In this case the dogs were trained to jump a fence when a whistle was blown and an electric shock administered at the same time. After five or six lessons, the dogs jumped the fence when the whistle was blown whether or not an electric shock was administered. And when the experiment was repeated four years later, one dog still jumped an imaginary fence at the sound of a whistle. And when he was confined in a pen where he was unable to jump, he showed signs of extreme anxiety at the sound of the whistle.

Now whilst we do not want to induce anxiety in our horses, it is important to know how it is induced, so that if we do come across any inexplicable fear or anxiety in a horse, we can attempt to trace it back to the unpleasant experience that caused it; and set out, taking time and patience, to retrain the animal until he no longer associates that particular thing with fear or pain.

Some time ago we carried out an experiment ourselves to test this process of association in horses, though we did not in this case induce fear, but hunger. We blew a whistle two minutes beforehand, every time we fed the horses. And within seven days, the horses were saying 'where's my bloody breakfast' as soon as the whistle was blown. It didn't matter what time of the day the whistle was blown, the horses still asked for food. And one horse continued to ask for food in response to the whistle after he had been turned out for three weeks.

The unconscious memory explains a lot of bad habits that can be found in horses: the horse may have forgotten the original situation that caused his fear, but the fear will still be there, and a similar situation years later may cause him great anxiety.

We had Jasmine as a two-year-old, and then later as a three-year-old. She was a sweet kind pony, but she used to wander around the yard a bit, getting in everyone's way, and stealing food where she could. Eventually she discovered that if the door of the feeding house was open, she could have a quick breakfast out of the feed barrel, which was a forty-gallon oil drum, before anyone discovered her.

On one particular occasion, she saw the door of the feeding house open, shot in, and dived into the feed barrel to have a quick breakfast. What she didn't know was that there was a hen in there already, also having a quick breakfast, and the hen, badly frightened, tried to fly out, and when it found the way barred, pecked Jasmine hard about the face and head. After that Jasmine never went into the feeding house again.

Jasmine was sold soon after that, but two years later, as a five-year-old, she was back with us. She came back rather late at night, and we put her into a loose box, where the manger was an oil drum three parts full of concrete. When I went out the next morning, however, I discovered that, though she was obviously hungry, she hadn't touched her feed. So I changed the feed, thinking that there was something wrong with it. She still wouldn't go near it, but I left her while I went in to have my breakfast. When I came out again and she still hadn't been near the feed, I just couldn't understand it. Then I remembered the incident of Jasmine and the hen. So I put the feed in the bucket, and she immediately ate it up. For the next three days I fed her in the bucket. At the end of the third day, I put the bucket into the drum for convenience, and again she wouldn't go anywhere near it: her one unpleasant experience with the hen, even after two years, still made her anxious about oil drums.

This is a typical example of how, once an animal has been badly frightened, behaviour can be affected over a period of years, and the damage once done can be very difficult to undo.

A horse that is apparently unreasonably nervous or frightened may also be generalizing from a different, but similar, situation he has encountered in the past: when a horse has learned a certain response to one situation, he may respond to all similar situations in the same way. Thus if a horse has had a pleasant experience when being ridden, he will look upon being ridden as a pleasant pastime; but if on the other hand he has been frightened when being ridden, he will tend to be nervous and upset whenever anyone gets on his back. And his current owner may be quite unaware of the reason.

Sometimes, if a horse has been badly treated by a man, he will be quite easy to handle by a woman, and go quietly and gently for her. But if he is ridden and handled by another man, even a gentle and sensitive rider, he may show signs of nervousness and anxiety, because he is associating men with pain.

The point to remember when training a horse, as I have already insisted, is that anything that frightens and upsets him, or is painful in any way, will be remembered for a very long time. And I can't stress enough how important it is that a horse should never be frightened or upset in his own particular stable: that he must have a place where he feels absolutely secure and safe. So if you have anything unpleasant to do with a horse, shoeing him, for instance, if he is difficult to shoe, never do it in his own loose box. Move him into another one. If you have to do something that is either painful to the horse, or likely to frighten him, always move him into a different stable so that he never associates pain or fear with his own stall.

If we are to keep our relations with our horses friendly and co-operative, it is also of course important to be able to recognize other emotional states than fear and anger. A horse doesn't feel the same all the time: from day to day, from hour to hour, his emotions will change. He may be happy, depressed, as well as afraid or angry. For the horse, like us, is affected by a large number of experiences, and it is extremely important that we should be able to identify each emotion as it shows, because it will affect the behaviour of the horse.

The classical reaction of a horse is what might be called the 'startle' pattern. You can observe this for yourself by tiptoeing up behind a horse, and clapping your hands. The reaction you will get is a startle: he will look towards the sound, open his mouth slightly, thrust his head and neck forward, and as his legs bend ever so slightly, his muscles will become tense. The uniformity of this response from one horse to another suggests that it is an inborn response, modified very little by learning or training.

Another stereotype response more regularly seen in animals than in people is the orientating response. This is a term that is applied to a horse that is orientating itself to a new stimulus or stimulus change. It involves tensing the muscles, and changing the position of the head, which in a horse is very similar to the startle pattern, except that the muscle tensing typically raises the head and tail, and draws the feet together. You can see this if you walk into a horse's loose box at night and turn the light on suddenly. The main difference from the startle pattern is that the startle pattern will prepare the horse for flight, whereas the orientating response does not prepare it for flight.

Other emotional responses vary from one horse to another. Each individual has his own way of expressing himself, but once you know your horses you will be able to interpret what emotions they are showing from their postures, gestures, and possibly also the sounds they make. Reading these signs comes into the field of equine communication, which I have dealt with in my book *Talking with Horses*, and it is a skill that anyone can learn.

In the horse there are only a few instinctive automatic responses that are inherited, and therefore universal: blinking the eye in response to change of light, flinching in response to pain, a salivary response to food it shares with human beings. And we all know the movement of the ear in response to variation in sound. But if you are trying to interpret a particular horse's emotions, you will have to get to know it as an individual, for its behaviour will be its own.

For example, Biddy shows affection by rubbing me with her nose, while Rostellan shows affection to my wife by catching hold of her sleeve between his lips. Rostellan shows fear by pricking his ears, and looking at the object, but Biddy shows fear by turning her head slightly to one side, putting her ears back, and raising one hind leg. Each horse says 'I am angry,' 'I am frightened,' or 'I am pleased' in his own particular way.

Some horses have extremely quick reactions. Jezebel's anger

for example explodes like a bomb into an aggressive movement, and it happens in a twinkling of an eye. While other more placid animals react slowly, giving you warning signs as the emotion builds up. The easiest way to interpret a horse's emotions is to observe him over a period of time in basic situations, and you will very quickly be able to discover how a horse shows his emotion, and exactly what emotion he is showing. Once you know whether he is pleased, enjoying himself or angry and frightened, you will know how to proceed in teaching him. For instance, if a horse when you pop him at a fence shows he is enjoying it, you can proceed quite happily. But if he is a little bit nervous and frightened you have to proceed slowly and very carefully, and build him up until he is enjoying what he is doing. If he is sullen and hostile, you must use patience and understanding to remove the hostility before you can hope to get him to enjoy himself.

It is of course the horses of strong emotion, and strong but nervous character, that can be most rewarding. They are a challenge, like Jezebel.

She, it will be remembered, was at one time considered to be completely unrideable and unmanageable. I had not had her very long when I decided to take her into a cross-country and dressage competition. This was a little ambitious since Jezebel had never done any dressage in her life, and her only schooling was conducted in the half-hour before we were due into the arena, at a canter. Already Jezebel was quite sure we were going to race and jump – she could feel that I was keyed up inside. So she either stood still, or set off at a strong canter when what I was trying to do was to get her to walk. At one time I thought I might risk a trot, and she responded by going absolutely flat-out in a circle. So the state of my nerves must be imagined when the time came for us to go into the dressage arena. We came up to the entrance of the arena at a brisk canter, with me expecting to do the fastest dressage test ever accomplished: I thought we might do most of it in about thirty seconds flat. Yet as we approached the entrance she changed her deportment completely. Instead of holding her head at an angle of forty-five degrees, looking straight up at the sky, she carried it straight, with her neck in the perfect arch. And she dropped back into a trot. We came to the centre of the arena, and she halted at the exact spot, whilst I saluted the judge, then went off at a very nice working trot and completed the test superbly: trotting when she should, walking when she should, cantering when she should, and ending up with only thirty-five penalties. This put her into fourth position.

We had a fair wait until the cross-country sections, and I had the opportunity to walk the course, and observe that most of the fences were young tree trunks which had been fastened to substantial gate-posts. This didn't do anything for my self-confidence. Expecting a twelve-two pony to carry twelve stone a mile and a half over three-foot-six fences, some of which had a four-foot spread, was asking a little bit much. But, since I had entered, I thought we had better make an attempt at least. So I got Jezebel down to the start in very good time and walked her round slowly. Her earlier desire to gallop when I wanted her steady had completely disappeared, and she walked round in what was for her such a civilized manner that I was able to light a cigarette, which helped me relax a little bit. We went up to the starting line: ten, nine, eight, seven, six, five, four, three, two, one, and we were away.

Jezebel went off like a bullet, and I had strong fears of disappearing over her tail. When I managed to get back into the saddle we were over the first fence, which was an easy one. Straight over a bank into fence two, a three-foot sharks teeth. And fence three, a gate. Jezebel was sailing. I knew that when riding Jezebel, like many very strong, very keen horses, it was a mistake to try and steady her, because she just takes hold and goes faster. So, I gave her all the rein she wanted and all the time she wanted. And this had the effect of steadying her a little bit. After that I didn't touch the reins at all, just calming her with my voice, and she jumped every fence immaculately. We finished up with the third fastest time of the day – which put me up into third place.

The only two horses to beat me were both sixteen-two thoroughbreds, and established eventers. The point is that I had complete empathy with Jezebel. All I had to do was to point her at the next fence, helping her with my weight all I could, but leaving it entirely to her to judge her distances, and her speed. I just talked to her all the time: 'Steady darling, steady darling, steady my beautiful. Now take it easy. Here we are going up-hill . . .' encouraging her all the time with my voice. When we pulled up, she had given everything. As soon as I got over the finishing line I got off her, and she stood and she panted and heaved for a good five minutes before she was able to walk away.

Ten minutes later she was as fresh as a daisy again. I got someone else to walk her round because I was too exhausted, and after a while I wandered over to tell her how clever and how good she was. She showed her affection by rubbing her head up and down to scratch her ears against my shoulder, so I caught hold of one ear and pulled it affectionately – thus abusing my privilege, because she took a sharp nip out of my arm and told me to behave myself.

10: *Dealing With Conflict*

Conflict arises within the horse who has two or more simultaneous needs, both of which cannot be satisfied at the same time. This causes one of the motives to be frustrated. And if one of the things that is frustrated is fear, this will make the horse anxious.

Of course the number of possible conflicts of motives that a horse can meet is enormous. The best and most common example of conflict, perhaps, arises in the horse that is reluctant to be caught. If you take a bucket of nuts into the field with you, the horse knows that you have food in the bucket. But he also knows that you want to catch him. And immediately a conflict arises between his greed for the nuts, on the one hand, and his reluctance to be caught on the other. If he satisfies his hunger, he is caught. If he stays free, he stays hungry.

Eventually of course, if you go about it the right way, he will come over to eat out of the bucket, and you will catch him. So you have frustrated his desire to be free. Now this is quite simple and straightforward if, once he is caught, the horse quite enjoys his work anyway. But if when you ride him he is frightened, or hurts himself jumping, next time you go to catch him you will have conflict not between two motives – greed and a wish to remain free – but three. You will have to contend also with the anxiety and nervousness caused by being frightened last time he was caught and ridden.

This sort of minor conflict arises very often in working with horses. But at times you may come across a major conflict between two powerful fears. If a horse is afraid of hurting himself jumping, and there is someone standing behind him with a dirty great hunting crop, the conflict of fears will be between hurting himself jumping and getting belted with the hunting crop. If the

fear of hurting himself jumping is not very great, and his fear of
the hunting crop is enormous, then he will jump the fence. But
if on the other hand he is equally afraid of both, he is going to
make a mess of jumping the fence, and so hurt himself more, so
that the next time, in spite of the hunting crop, he will refuse to
jump altogether. This is a conflict of two very great fears, and it
can be very damaging.

If on the other hand he bundled over the fence somehow,
hurting himself only a little, he will jump it again next time because he must. But as soon as the hunting crop is taken away,
he will refuse to jump. And after that he will look upon jumping
as something that is unpleasant and frightening. He is likely to
display a complete revulsion against crossing any form of obstacle, and it is only by resolving this fear with sympathy and
understanding that he will be encouraged to jump again willingly.

In a situation like this, the first and most important thing to
do is to get the horse to enjoy jumping again. The best way to
do this is to let him follow other horses over a series of low
obstacles, two-foot or two-foot-three are high enough. When he
is enjoying galloping and jumping with the other horses, you can
send the other horses on in front, and when they are at the other
end of the jumps he will be tearing to get at them so he will actually enjoy jumping the fences.

Similarly you can pop over a few low fences when he is going
home to his dinner. Then when he is jumping low obstacles
happily to get to other horses, or on his way home, you can take
him out by himself and let him jump the same obstacles alone.
You do not want to change the height of the jumps until he is
jumping the low fences every day with enthusiasm and pleasure.
You will know when this is because when he comes to the first
fence he will be reaching for the bit and saying 'come let's get
going'. You can then raise the fences two or three inches. Or you
can introduce a new jump, always making sure that anything he
jumps he is going to enjoy jumping. It's a very long and slow
process. Depending upon how frightened and upset he was

originally, it can take anything from six months to three years before you get back to jumping really big strong fences in competition. As in all things with horses, and especially in retraining, there is no quick way, there is no short cut. At the same time it must be remembered that boredom is something that will cut right across his training programme – this again will involve a conflict of emotions, the feeling of dull monotony conflicting with his desire to do what you want.

The art of handling any conflict between one set of desires in a horse and another, is to eliminate the cause: for example, if the conflict is between his boredom with his work and his desire to please you, varying the work so that he is no longer bored will eliminate the conflict altogether. Since when a horse says that he won't or can't do something, you have to stay there until he does it happily and willingly for you – if you ever hope to work successfully with that horse again – as the horse is bigger and stronger than you are, this is often the *only* way of dealing with conflict.

An example of such a technique arose in our work with a yearling sent to us because, among other things, he was impossible to load into a trailer or a lorry. So the first thing we did was slowly, patiently and determinedly to train him to accept the lorry. This involved, first, coaxing him with some nuts, second, moving his legs forward one at a time, and finally two people pushing him hard from behind.

When we eventually got him on to the lorry – it took us about forty minutes – we made a tremendous fuss of him, gave him a few nuts and took him out again. Then we put him back on the lorry again, which this time took us a quarter of an hour or twenty minutes. When he was in, he had a few nuts, was brought out again, and loaded straight back in again. This time the process took only about five minutes. By the time we had finished, we were leading him in and out of the lorry with no trouble whatever.

This problem had arisen from sheer bloody-mindedness on his part, which made his owner a little bit frightened of him, and angry. So he got walloped and this compounded his fear, until he was impossible to load. Such a conflict could be resolved only by:

(a) removing his fear of being loaded – at no time when we were doing this did anyone raise a voice, and at no time was he hit;

(b) making him realize that when he got into the lorry he would be made a fuss of, and fed;

(c) impressing on him that whether he was difficult or easy, he had to go into the lorry anyway.

For the next week, he was fed only when he was in the lorry. And at the end of the week, you only had to drop the tail board of the lorry and he was straight into it shouting 'where is my bloody breakfast'.

We had thus changed his attitude completely within a week. From flatly refusing to go near the lorry at all, he was so anxious to do so that the one thing he wanted in the world was to get into the lorry and have a feed.

This epitomizes the whole essence of training a horse, which is not getting a horse to do a thing because he has to, though you may have to do this to start with. It is getting a horse to do a thing because he *wants* to – changing his wishes and desires so that by allowing him to do what *he* wants, you will be getting him to do what you want. The bond he has with you will be all the greater, as jumping a fence or exercising or schooling becomes a reward in itself because he enjoys doing it. And you are increasing his enjoyment each time you do it.

Two forms of behaviour are typical of the problems that arise from conflict in the motivations of the horse. One is what might be termed avoidance behaviour, manifested for example in the horse who goes into a fence 'will I,' 'won't I,' 'can I,' and at the last moment refuses to jump, or attempts to jump and makes a mess of it. This avoidance will be far worse the next time and every succeeding time he tries, unless tackled immediately. Another type of avoidance involves bucking the rider off, bolting, or refusing to go near the fence altogether.

Such a conflict problem faced me three years ago, and caused great mirth locally. A friend who has hunting hounds had a nice little fourteen-two chestnut mare named Robbie that he wanted to hunt hounds off, and he offered to lend her to me for a few days to get her going quietly before he hunted her himself. I'd had the mare for some time, and she was going quietly and gently – she was an extremely good and willing jumper – when we attended a very big lawn meet. I got on her, and hounds were unloaded, and I noticed she was going a little bit crab-like, and had her back up. But I thought this was because she hadn't done much work recently, and was just feeling full of herself. We proceeded on to the lawn of the house, and as I attended to the hounds, keeping them under control, I noticed that she was flicking her ears, swishing her tail, and half threatening to kick. I got myself set in the saddle ready for trouble, but I wasn't quite quick enough. She exploded into three gigantic bucks, and I did a neat parabola in the air, landing on my backside in the middle of the hounds.

I got back on her and managed to keep her from bucking for the next ten minutes, keeping her head well up and my backside well down in the saddle. But while everyone else was drinking and speechifying, the hounds moved off to the first draw. As soon as she felt grass under her feet, I was on the ground again. I mounted a third time and we went on to draw following a sheep path alongside the mountain on a very steep slope. We hadn't gone fifty or a hundred yards before she suddenly turned straight down the hill, bucking as she went, and I didn't stand a chance. Again I executed three somersaults, disappearing from view into a patch of bracken whilst Robbie proceeded bucking on her way. Whipping into hounds isn't the time to have a battle with a horse. Fortunately I had lent my own horse to a friend of mine for the day, so I gave him Robbie and took my horse back, and proceeded to have a very good day's hunting.

Apart from having to listen to my various so-called friends making suggestions that I should take riding lessons, and asking when I was going to put on another rodeo performance, I was

not much damaged so I arranged with the owner of Robbie to
have her delivered to me the next day. As soon as I had had my
Sunday lunch, I went out and put saddle and bridle on her and
took her out. She had one minor go at bucking, but that was all.
She didn't make another mistake. After that I had her out every
day, working her gently, cantering, jumping and no trouble at all.
A month later I thought she was going so sweetly and kindly, I
would amaze everyone with the transformation in her, and took
her hunting again. But to make quite sure, we stopped the Land
Rover and trailer a couple of miles from the Meet and rode the
last two miles, Robbie going very sweetly. Unfortunately the
Huntsman had had trouble starting his Land Rover that
morning, so he was half-an-hour late, and I sat on Robbie,
talking to various people at the Meet about how quiet and easy
she was.

The Huntsman arrived eventually, got his horse out of the
trailer, and let hounds go. Immediately Robbie exploded into
a buck. I rode her for the next hour keeping a very tight rein
on her, but the whole time she was attempting to buck, and every
time hounds came near her her ears started flicking, and her tail
started swishing.

Otherwise a completely sweet and easy horse to ride, it seemed
Robbie would become a devil incarnate when she saw hounds. I
don't know why – she may have been a member of the League
against Cruel Sports. To this day I am completely mystified. She
is the only horse that I have ever come across who didn't love
hunting.

A further avoidance technique a horse will use, apart from
bucking, bolting, and refusing to go near the obstacle, is rearing.
This is caused either by fear of a particular object or experience,
or by bad handling on the part of her rider.

All vices can be overcome with time and patience provided
of course that the vice you are trying to eliminate is worth the
time and patience involved in tackling it. If, for example, I had
persevered for two or three months hunting Robbie, I could
eventually have got her hunting, in a reasonable manner if some-

what reluctantly. And in time no doubt she would have come to enjoy it, since she was an extremely good ride, and a very good little jumper. But it was much simpler to hunt something else that wanted to hunt – it is much more fun hunting a horse that's mad to get after hounds than the one that isn't particularly enthusiastic. And in Robbie's case, she was a superb little hack, very quiet and gentle, and it was thought it would be a very great pity to get into a major conflict with her, and possibly sour her very sweet nature, merely to turn her into a reluctant hunter. Other than in the hunting field she never thought about bucking or misbehaving.

Anger and hostility in a horse is almost always caused by interference. A horse that is by himself in a field cannot get angry or hostile. Even a subordinate horse within a herd will never show anger or hostility to one of the herd leaders, and similarly the herd leader will not show anger or hostility – until he is interfered with by another horse. But as soon as something interferes with him, anger, fear, or hostility can be aroused. The whole essence of our training must be to avoid anger and hostility. We go to a lot of trouble to do so.

This can be done in two ways: either by training the horse in such a way that we give him so much pleasure and excitement that the question of rebellion does not arise; or by repeating a controversial action so often that habit replaces anger and hostility.

We use such techniques when we are gentling a horse. We take him out with other horses so that he is so much enjoying being with other horses that he forgets to resent being ridden: equates being ridden with enjoying himself. He will very quickly look on the sight of his bridle and saddle with pleasure, because he expects that when they are on he will enjoy himself. On the other hand, when we have to make a horse pick up his feet, which he finds it very hard to do willingly, we use the other strategy, of simple repetition to create a habit. All horses have a firm idea that their four feet are meant to be kept on the ground, and they get annoyed to a greater or a lesser extent as soon as you try to pick them up. But if you constantly pick up the horse's feet, he becomes accustomed to having his feet picked up, and the more often you do it the less notice he will take. You will eventually get to the stage where as soon as you touch his fetlock he will lift it up himself. Repetition in fact has reduced the original anger and hostility at having his feet picked up to nil.

Few people welcome anger and hostility in their horses, even when they sympathize with their fear and frustrations. They recognize that anger produces a cycle of action and reaction that is very difficult to escape from: when a horse gets angry, people tend to feel threatened by them. This makes them frightened, and to hide this fear they will probably stimulate more anger by shouting, or threatening with a stick. This of course increases the fear within the horse, so that the horse himself will feel threatened, and so the cycle continues.

In actual fact the easiest way to extinguish anger and fear in a horse is by calmness and determination. If you are calm and quiet with a horse, no matter how frightened and angry it is, the horse will tend to become less frightened, and less angry. The last thing on earth to do is to shout and brandish a stick, or to try to punish him in any way for his fear.

Just after Christmas I was called in to handle a difficult and unmanageable horse. She kicked very badly. As soon as you went into her stable, she would go into the far corner and present you with her backside, and if you went near her she would kick out at you with one leg. Even when you got to her head she would kick forward, something I have seen only once in a horse before. She caught me with her hind leg when I was standing by her front leg. But I just talked to her quietly and gave her a few oats every time she turned her head towards me. In about half an hour I could walk up to her and put my hand over her neck, without her kicking me. Then I put a saddle on her. As soon as I went to fasten up the girth, she kicked again. But again talking quietly and slowly, I eventually got her so that I could fasten the girth without too much trouble. Her previous experience of course was that every time she presented her backside she had got hit, which started her kicking, which in turn made her owner more and more frightened of her. This meant that in effect she was getting away with kicking her owner, and getting her own way. But by quiet determination I taught her in a very short time that I was going to catch her, that I wasn't afraid of her, and that when she did come round she would get rewarded with a few oats. The motive behind her behaviour was thus changed very quickly from a desire not to be caught to a desire to get caught in order to be made a fuss of, and have a few oats.

However, if I had been aggressive with her, indeed if I had raised my voice above the quiet sing-song note, she would immediately have been frightened and terrified, presented her hind-quarters to me again, and no doubt kicked me hard in a tender spot to teach me to behave better next time.

We must thus always suppress the anger within ourselves when reacting with horses. We know that it will only evoke the expression of more anger, and more fear in our horses. We must stay cool and quiet. This state of affairs is no doubt extremely frustrating to the horse: anger is a momentary and very immediate emotion in a horse, that needs to be vented immediately, so when he is all set for a battle, he must feel extremely frustrated if he is causing no response in you. But in due course he will calm down. On the other hand if you punish anger in a horse, you are only giving him another cause to be angry, and increasing his fear – which is usually the initial cause of the anger – and he will react until he is beyond your control, and his own.

If a horse is frightened by something in a hedge, and you, his rider, punish him, instead of curing the vice of shying you may be increasing his fear of the object. You are in effect justifying his fear: he shied at a paper bag, and he got hurt at the same time, so he will equate being hurt with the paper bag. His rider could quite conceivably be making the vice worse by increasing his fear and nervousness. The best that suppressing the anger in a horse by punishment can achieve is to teach the horse not to *show*

his anger, and you end up with a sullen, bad tempered and un-
willing horse who is by countless means avoiding doing what you
want.

Some people find themselves at odds with their horse because
they are trying to force him into a mould that the horse is un-
suited for, either temperamentally or physically. Or it may be that
weakness in the rider allows the horse to misbehave. A horse may
go quite sweetly for one person and be nearly unrideable by
another.

Fear and anger and frustration are the causes of most of the
vices that develop in horses. And anger is the thing that most
people are least able to deal with. When the anger within the
horse is suppressed it is the frustration of the anger that causes
the awkwardness and bloody-mindedness. If a horse has been
accustomed to doing something, and you stop him, his automatic
reaction is bound to be 'Why the bloody hell shouldn't I? I have
always done it.' And if you respond to this by saying, 'You
aren't doing it because I damned well say you aren't', you immediately land yourself in the classical situation of conflict. If
the horse then does what he originally wanted to do, and you let
him do it, he has established a position of dominance over you by
a display of anger, and will be encouraged to display anger on
future occasions when he wants his own way. If on the other hand
you stop him doing what he wants to do, and establish your
position of dominance over him, you are going to be little better
off, because he is just going to be sullen and bad-tempered over
the whole incident. And if you punish him severely in the
process of stopping him doing what he wanted to do, he is
going to be not only angry and sullen: he is also going to be
frightened.

If on the other hand your reaction to his 'Why the hell shouldn't
I?' is 'Because we are going to do so-and-so instead, and you are
going to enjoy it', then he will accept the change quite willingly
and happily.

Imagine, for example, that a horse has refused to take off from
the ground with his previous owner. You present him with a

three-foot-six fence, going away from home. You can make him jump the fence by flogging him over it with a hunting crop, but he will end up afterwards disliking jumping, disliking you, and a little bit frightened of you as well. Or you can allow him not to jump the fence, and he will have established his dominance over you.

On the other hand, you could put up a small fence on your way home. And when you come to the fence, when he says, 'Oh, I don't jump fences. I can't jump fences,' you could say to him 'You are going to jump the fence because this is the way we go home to dinner.' He will scramble over the fence, and find he gets home to dinner. And the next day when you come to the same fence, he will scramble over it a little bit more easily. At the end of the week when you come up to it on your way home, he will pop over it quite happily.

It must be remembered that there is a great deal of difference between allowing a horse to do what he wants, and getting the horse to want to do what you want him to. They are two completely different things, as diametrically opposite as getting a horse to do what you want him to do and making him do something that he has bloody well got to.

Most people when training a horse tend to concentrate on the *suppression* of his anger. But the real skill, especially in the early stages, is to avoid any situation that would lead to anger. So in our work we lay the emphasis on getting the horse to enjoy himself. But of course, when we are riding a horse constantly, we are bound at some time to come across a situation where the horse refuses to do what we ask him to. And then we must make our stand, with patience, and if necessary with a smack, but not too much of the smack, we insist that the horse do what we tell him to. And then when he does that, we tell him what a clever horse he is.

Teaching Jack to jump was a challenge that might well have been mishandled if we had ever decided to confront it head-on. We had Jack for four or five years, and he solidly refused to jump. But since he was a fantastic riding pony, we didn't bother

to teach him – we had plenty of horses who wanted to jump anyway, and for us it is seldom worth spending time on making a
horse jump who doesn't want to. Then one day we were out
riding and there was a tree laying across the track. As soon as they
saw it all the other horses pricked their ears, cantered into it, and
popped over. It was only about eighteen inches high. Jack in his
hurry to catch up with the other horses forsook the principles
of a lifetime, and took off, all feet off the ground at the same
time. We made such a fuss of him that he must have felt he
had jumped a fence at least twice as big as Beechers Brook.
And after that, whenever there was an obstacle in the way on
the ride, instead of going round it Jack jumped over it. And
within about six weeks Jack was jumping everything quite happily
and well.

Of course we could have *made* Jack jump much earlier, but
it would have entailed a battle. Our work involves teaching people
who have never jumped, to jump, so we have to have horses who
jump willingly and well, and basically this means horses whose
one desire in life is to jump, not horses that have been taught to
jump reluctantly. A sullen and frustrated horse is not a good
and happy companion. In general, then, the rule is that it is
much better to avoid conflict where possible.

I always try to avoid head-on battles with horses, except on
grounds of my own choosing. For example, if I have a horse sent
to me that is a very bad bucker, I will do all I can to avoid doing
anything that makes him buck until I come to the bottom of a
steep hill. Then I point him up the hill, driving my heels in,
and saying: 'Right, go on you beggar, buck!' And every time he
lands, I drive my heels in and say: 'Go on, good boy, buck again.'
By the time he has gone half way up a steep hill, the effort of
bucking and failing to dislodge me from the saddle seems more
and more pointless, so he stops bucking. I find, if I do this four
or five times, all desire to buck vanishes, and in future that horse
will buck only out of *joie de vivre*. Just occasionally, however,
you start something, as I did with Boyo, not realizing that you
are going to have a pitched battle, but then, having started, you

must finish what you are doing. You must finish it, or you don't go home.

Most, if not all, shades of emotion are a combination of feelings: fear is often mixed with anger, just as it can also be mixed with pleasure. And if a horse is frightened, and you make him do something he doesn't want to do, his fear will change to anger at you for trying to make him do it.

Twenty years ago, when we first had the Bishop and he had just recently been gentled, I took him out exercising one day. It was about two hours' ride, going in a circle from the yard, and I intended to get back to the yard just before dinner. Twenty yards from the stable was a ford across a small stream however, which we had to cross to get back into the yard. What I didn't know when I chose the route was that the Bishop had never crossed water in his life. So when we got to the stream, he stopped dead. I tried to coax him forward and he took two steps to one side. I coaxed him again and he took two steps to the other side. So we went on, with me getting more forceful, and his reaction to my forcefulness increasingly acrobatic: he reared and bucked, plunged, did everything except go forward across that stream. His initial fear of crossing the water had combined with anger at being asked to do something that he had never done before, and which he thought dangerous, if not impossible. As a result I didn't get my dinner that day until half-past three.

I had to stay there, coaxing and talking, until I had eventually calmed him down. Then he put one foot in the water, quite by accident, and when he had discovered that the foot hadn't disappeared, and it wasn't painful, I coaxed him forward again, and he put it in again. Again it didn't disappear and so with great courage he put another foot in the water. He stood like that for at least five minutes. Then I managed to coax him forward half a step, then another half a step, until eventually he had all four feet in the water. This was too much for the Bishop. He stood there trembling for a couple of minutes, then he spun round and was flat out back up the way we had come. I steadied him and walked him back down to the river. This time he walked in with two front feet, and finding it quite pleasant, decided to take a big stride forward. But as the next foot hit the water a drop splashed up and hit him on the nose. This again was altogether too much, so he he decided to get rid of me, and he arched his back and went into a terrific buck.

Fortunately it was in the right direction. He landed with all four feet in the water, the shock of the splash sent him into another buck, and this took us out and up the other side. I rode up to the yard to collect my wife, who jumped on Cork Beg, and we rode back down to the stream. Cork Beg was being asked to act as schoolmaster, so he splashed through the water. The Bishop, seeing Cork Beg go across without thinking anything of it, tried to jump the stream in one, but landed in the middle again and splashed his tummy. However, when we got to the other side, Cork Beg turned round and went back across the river, and the Bishop very gently followed. Thus we walked back and forward twenty or thirty times, until the Bishop had finally accepted the fact that crossing the river was neither dangerous nor impossible. Then with great thankfulness we went back up to the stables, unsaddled the Bishop, and gave him and Cork Beg a feed. And I went to my very dry and very tasteless dinner.

From these two instances it must not be thought that I am perpetually having battles with my horses at the wrong time. I am not. I have remarkably few battles with my horses. But when a battle is forced on you, you have to go through with it. And those are the battles that always stand out in your mind. Not only do you remember the battle, you remember your empty stomach as well!

Of course, if I had realized that the Bishop had never crossed water, or that he was afraid of water, I should have led him across the water, following two or three other horses, in the first place. And I would have avoided a battle. After seeing the other horses cross the water, the Bishop would have crossed without any difficulty at all. We are perpetually looking for ways round conflict, for a battle is of little use to anybody. All it does is upset you and upset your time schedule – and if you are as busy as I am, you have a very tight time schedule. And they set back the work you have been doing on the horse by days, weeks and sometimes even months.

11: *Practical Applications of Horse Psychology*

Pure knowledge to the scientist may be an end in itself, but to the practical horseman it is pointless unless use can be made of it. And it is only of use with horses if it does one of four things:

first, if it increases the wellbeing of the horse;

second, if it makes the horse's work easier for it to perform;

third, if it improves its performance, not only in competition but in quite simple hacking and riding;

and last, if it increases the owner's enjoyment of the horse, and improves his riding ability.

These four conditions are like a pyramid. The horse's wellbeing makes it possible for his work to become easier, because unless he is strong and fit his work is bound to be hard and tedious. And if you have a fit well horse it is important to make the most of him, which in turn is bound to improve his performance, and of course if the horse's performance improves, his rider's enjoyment will increase automatically.

The first task, then, is to make sure of the horse's physical wellbeing. The most important thing is to know what its basic needs are. The experts tend to lay down rules: they say that a horse of certain such a size, doing such and such work, needs X pounds of food. And I can state quite categorically that this is wrong. Each horse is an individual with his own individual likes and dislikes, and his own individual needs. It may well be that the average horse, say of fourteen-two to fifteen hands, doing a reasonable amount of work, needs on an average twelve pounds of corn and twenty pounds of hay a day. But unfortunately I have never come across an average horse, just as I have never met an average man – who no doubt would be a mixture of black, white, yellow and various shades of khaki, but I wouldn't know him if I saw him anyway. I've only come across individuals, and there is no way I know of assessing an individual's needs except to get to know him.

Let us start by finding out how much water he needs. This isn't just a question of finding out what his total requirement of water is, but of how also he likes to drink it: a small or large amount of water at what time of the day. For example, Rostellan normally drinks about six gallons of water a day, but when he comes back from hunting or show-jumping he will drink six gallons of water in the space of about three or four hours. This isn't just because he has been sweating: he requires water to relax him physically and mentally.

I know from my own experience that when I am riding in a race my mouth goes dry, and after a race I am always thirsty, even if I have fallen off at the first fence, and taken very little out of myself. I've probably passed a great deal of urine before racing, from excitement, and this water has to be replaced. And it is exactly the same thing with Rostellan. If we know what his increased requirement of water is after hunting, we can meet the requirement. If on the other hand we don't know that he has an increased need for water after being out, we could quite happily put his normal ration of water in his stall, leaving him thirsty.

The same principle – familiarity with individual needs – applies to the feeding of a horse. The first thing you need to know is the amount of food he requires to maintain his bodyweight, given the work he is doing. This may be the average amount of food prescribed by the text book, or it may be two or three pounds more, or two or three pounds less, depending upon his abilities as a food converter. But on top of this it is also necessary to know exactly what his greed factor is: just how much more food he will eat given a chance. This information can be of use in two or three ways.

If he is an extremely greedy horse, and has a greed factor that will make him eat eight, ten, or twelve pounds more than his ration, you can then of course use his greed to make him perform better, that is, you can use food as a powerful reward. But it is far more important to know that he is a shy or difficult feeder, or if he tends to refuse to eat after competition, because this knowledge not only helps you in feeding him, it also tells you something about his degree of nervous tension, the build-up within him if he is hunting or competing. It may then be necessary to resort to all sorts of subterfuges before competing to get the best out of him.

Molfre was a typical example of this. The day before racing, if he knew he was going to race, he would tend to eat only half his feed, and he would sweat. The build-up of tension also meant that he was sweating up long before you got to the race course. We overcame this tension within him in two ways. First, we made no preparation the day before racing. We didn't give him any extra grooming or tidying up, or trim his mane or tail. Second, I would load him into the trailer just in his night rug; and on non-racing days I'd take him out for a drive in the trailer in exactly the same way – just drive round the mountain for half an hour, bring him back and unload him. By this strategy he never knew whether he was going racing until he actually got on to the race course. We had relieved his tension and he hadn't taken a lot out of himself before he got to the meeting.

To show the variation in the needs of different horses for food, I have only to look at the three horses that we have been hunting this winter: Rostellan, Clancy and Charlie. All three have been having the equivalent of fifteen pounds of corn per day, although Rostellan and Clancy have been hunting on an average three days a fortnight, and Charlie has been hunting only about three days a month. At the beginning of winter they were all approximately of the same bodyweight, Charlie being an inch taller than Clancy, and Clancy an inch taller than Rostellan. So in theory they all needed approximately the same amount of food. Yet Rostellan has been putting on condition slowly all winter as he built up and muscled up; Clancy has maintained his bodyweight, certainly hasn't lost any condition, and has put on an awful lot of muscle; whilst Charlie has been losing weight all winter. This has proved very difficult to correct, because whilst both Rostellan and Clancy would have eaten half as much again as we were feeding them, we were feeding Charlie right up to the limit of his consumption, right through the winter. The real reason for his loss of bodyweight, we concluded, was that it was taking him a very long time to settle down psychologically after five years in training. For not only had we disrupted what were for him the habits of a lifetime, we were demanding new and different things of him, which brought new and different needs and drives into play. He didn't relax, and was still not happy until we had had him nearly six weeks. But once he had relaxed and started realizing what was required of him, and enjoying the work that he was doing, he stopped losing bodyweight, and over two or three weeks he started putting on condition again.

I can even put a date on the day he started putting on condition. He hadn't been going at all well out hunting, being surly and bad tempered. That day, January 7th, we had an extremely long run from Drefach and it took me a very long time to find hounds. Then about half-way through the day Charlie suddenly settled down and started working well, and by the time I had found hounds and got back, and I met the Land Rover and trailer coming to look for me, Charlie was so tired he could hardly lift one foot after another. But he seemed contented with himself. Of course after a hard day's hunting like that, he went back to looking an absolute skeleton and he hardly touched his feed that night, or the following morning. Yet the following evening he ate up well. On the Friday morning after that I opened the stable doors, went back up the line of boxes to fetch the feeds, and I passed Charlie who put his head out and caught hold of the sleeve of my coat, and stopped me. I rubbed him between his ears, and scratched his chin. And he reciprocated by rubbing up and down on my shoulder nearly knocking me off my feet.

From that moment on, slowly and certainly, his attitude to his work became more and more cheerful. He became happier within himself, and he stopped losing condition. About a fortnight later he had quite clearly started improving.

This is an example where all the feeding charts in the world could be of no help at all, because the crucial factor was a psychological one. Emotional tensions can affect digestion and health. This can be verified by your own observations of your own horse: if you take him out and get him excited, you will immediately see him evacuating dung, and while he is under the stress of the excitement or nervousness, you will see the texture of his dung change. He will evacuate it much sooner. This is nature's way of accelerating his digestion preparatory to emptying his stomach for flight in the wild. Mental stress in fact can change the digestive processes of the horse completely, so that he is converting his food less efficiently – his food is shooting through his body like a moonshot through outer space. But once he becomes mentally relaxed, the whole digestive process will be slowed down so that he digests his food more thoroughly. So if you want a horse to digest his food efficiently, you have to get him mentally relaxed and well: to get your horse physically at the peak of his form, in other words, you must first get him mentally fit.

In particular he must be mentally and physically relaxed in his stable, because not only will this promote his digestion, it will also help him to recharge himself mentally and physically for further endeavour.

After the needs for food and water, the next thing we must discover about our horses is the extent and nature of their sexual drives. These can have a considerable influence on their performance.

For the time being, anyway, we can ignore the sex drive of the stallion, since most of us don't ride stallions, and certainly most of us don't use one in competition. We ride geldings, or mares, and the drives of geldings, as I have already mentioned, will vary from horse to horse. Some geldings can be considerably affected by the presence of mares in season, to the extent of being distracted by them, which makes them either nappy or excitable and of course impairs performance. So it is extremely necessary to know what your horse's reactions are likely to be. Nothing is more annoying, after taking a horse fifty miles to a competition, than finding your gelding, instead of dazzling everyone with his ability, and leaving the crowd dumbfounded with admiration at yours, spending all his time shrieking at the top of his voice to a lady love; or when you come up to jump a fence he is so distracted by some seductive beauty that he goes straight through, and you land flat on your face.

Equally, a mare's performance will rise and fall with her sexual activity, usually reaching a peak midway between the times she becomes in season, and a trough when she is actually in season.

You will also be observing how much exercise your horse is taking in his stable, and how much movement his temperament requires, movement and light being as necessary for a horse as food and water. We explained earlier how you can measure the amount of movement a horse needs. The fat lazy horse is quite easily managed. Apart from the fact that you know that he needs a large amount of exercise to keep his spare tyre at a reasonable size, you don't have to worry very much about giving him mental activity. Stimulating him mentally is probably as difficult as stimulating him physically, and he may require an atom bomb to wake him up.

The horse that is walking round the stable like a caged lion, however, needs more careful handling. In the first place, it must be remembered that although he will not need very much exercise, he is also walking off the condition you are trying to put on him at great expense – mainly because he needs the mental stimulation that the movement is giving him. However, if you accept the fact that he is pacing round his stable either because his nerves are tense and the movement relieves the tension – in exactly the same way as when my nerves are on edge I like a glass of Guinness and a cigarette to relieve my tension – or because he is bored, you can begin to take remedial action.

Miracle cures for a horse of course do not exist. But it is possible to steady his nerves and to reduce his boredom. One remedy that has had some good results is playing music.

It is an established fact that milking cows let their milk down far more readily in the milking parlour if music is being played while they are milked. And we have observed with our own horses that some of them do enjoy listening to music, so if you could, you might put an expensive transistor into every box. But then some of your horses will be lovers of Brahms, and others will like pop music, and when the radio changed from Brahms to pop or vice versa, they may smash the radio. They are quite likely to smash the radio anyway, out of curiosity and boredom.

A far simpler way of providing mental stimulation for the horse is to make absolutely certain that at all times throughout daylight hours, he can see out of his loose box; not only to see out, but put his head out so that he can look to the left, look to the right, and gaze up at the sky at the aeroplanes if he wants to. Since all horses, like the Elephant's Child, are full of satiable curiosity, they will tend to spend a large part of the day looking out in case they miss something interesting. And if they are standing at the doorway looking out, they are not walking round their boxes and losing condition.

Once you have got to know something of your horse's physical needs and his temperament, you can set out to discover whether or not he is a free natural jumper, whether he does a good dressage test, whether he is a good hack, whether he's fast, whether he's competitive, whether he enjoys doing something for its own sake or whether he's an equine hippy with one desire in life – to live on Social Security and loaf around all day doing nothing.

It has always amazed me that while nobody would dream of trying to turn a tone-deaf individual like myself into an opera singer or a pianist, people will spend countless hours and endless energy trying to turn non-jumping horses into show jumpers, non-galloping horses into race horses, and shambling lazy individuals into dressage horses.

I must admit however that I'm in no position to throw stones, since I live in a glass house myself, spending a large amount of time trying to train horses that aren't fast enough to catch a cold to win point-to-points for me. And just occasionally I am very lucky with them – just often enough to make me keep on trying.

I had a typical example of this sort of luck at the East Devon point-to-point eighteen or nineteen years ago. I'd been asked to ride a very slow and ponderous hunter in the Cotley hunt race, and since I'd been booked to ride in every other race on the card that day, the only race I could ride Sandyboy in was the open. But whichever race he was in he was going to come last anyway, we reasoned, so we didn't let the fact that every other horse in the race was a very good point-to-pointer worry us.

The start of the East Devon in those days was just beyond the finishing post. And after the starter, who had the nickname among jockeys of Blind Bertie, had called the roll there were five minutes to wait for the start. A couple of the jockeys, to keep their mounts moving, rode back up into the crowd, whilst the others walked their horses round in a circle. Since my horse was going to need all the energy he could summon in the race, I stood by the starter and did not move. Suddenly Blind Bertie called the runners into line and, without bothering to see if everyone or even anyone, was there, he dropped his flag and away we went. The jockeys who weren't ready, including the two up in the crowd, spent the next two or three minutes arguing with Blind Bertie about whether or not he could start the race when they weren't ready, and by the time they realized that the race was on I had already jumped three fences.

Sandyboy was putting his best foot forward and going at least twice as fast as he had ever gone before in his life. We proceeded in this manner for two circuits and led the field all the way until just after the last fence. Unfortunately I was caught twenty yards from the winning post, beaten into second place mainly because Sandyboy had already given everything he had got and galloped himself into the ground. He could hardly totter over the winning line. But to get within two lengths of Gay Peri, in an open point-to-point, was no mean performance.

Some horses are lucky just as some people are. They simply seem to be born that way. On another occasion at the South

Dorset point-to-point, I rode another non-galloping horse who seemed to have the luck of the devil. Two very good horses had been brought down from the Mendip Hunt, and since nothing else was going in the open race, we slipped my horse in on the grounds that he was at least guaranteed third place.

The other two went off at a hell of a pace, while Rory and I went round in a very sedate manner, knowing we were getting a fiver for our pains, and enjoying a grandstand view of some beautiful riding and fencing by the two cracks. After we had gone two miles it wouldn't have been true to say that I couldn't see the others, but they were at least a fence in front of me. As we came round the Flagstaff, which was the corner into the straight, I saw them going hell for leather into the last fence and disappearing the other side. Then as we took off at our leisure at the last fence, I was rather surprised to see a somewhat silent crowd in front of me and no sign of the other two. Only when we came down and landed on the other side could I see why. One of the jockeys was sitting on the ground hammering it with his whip, and the other was lying recumbent with two ambulance men leaning over him trying to decide whether he was dead or only unconscious. I proceeded in solitary magnificence past a dumbfounded and silent crowd to a very welcome and unexpected winning reception.

Lucky occasions like this however are very few and far between, and it is infinitely better not to try and train a horse that doesn't want to jump for competition, or to make a dressage horse out of something that would be far happier pulling a plough.

So the first task is to find out the things a horse does well naturally and the things he wants to do. After that you start creating new things for him to want to do, and trying to extend his natural abilities. It is most important at this time to decide two things:

   (a) whether you are mentally compatible with your horse – whether you have that essential empathy that is necessary to get the fullest enjoyment out of him; and

   (b) whether the horse is suitable for your purpose.

What your desires are only you know; this is something you have to be honest about with yourself. Just because your friends are all dreaming of becoming Ann Moores and Marion Moulds, doesn't mean that you have to showjump. And because your grandfather's second cousin once rode round Aintree, doesn't mean that you have to ride point-to-pointing. It is what you want to do yourself that is important – what you enjoy doing.

If for example you feel the need to have a priest give you the last rites every time you have to jump a fence, don't jump. If you think that riding and racing is a very inefficient form of suicide, don't race. And if you think that dressage is something that should be confined to the circus ring, don't attempt to do dressage. You don't even have to ride the blasted things: some people get great pleasure out of keeping a horse just for its company – looking after him, grooming him, wandering out at night to chat with him when no one else will listen. But do make sure that the horse you have is one that naturally does the things that you want to do, and if it doesn't, get rid of it and get one that does. I'm not thinking of your wellbeing when I recommend this, but the horse's. There is nothing so frustrating for a good free jumper than being ridden by someone who is scared stiff going into a fence; and there is nothing so frustrating for a free active horse than being ridden by someone who wants to amble round the countryside, admiring the view. So if you want to jump, get a horse that jumps naturally. If on the other hand you want to sit on top of the hill admiring mother nature, get a horse that is quite happy to go to sleep while you do so.

Once having got a horse that wants to do the same things as you do, you have to start to extend his abilities. The basic component of all riding is hacking. It doesn't matter what form of equestrianism you are going in for, three-quarters of the time at least you will be doing nothing but walking and trotting on the road. And it doesn't matter whether you have a race horse, a dressage horse, a showjumper or an eventer, the basis of all this work is fitness Fitness is achieved by exercise, by walking and trotting, and this is the thing that you will be doing most. It is essential that the horse should do it well; so you school him.

Now schooling has two aspects:

first, you are trying to accustom him to good habits so that he does the right thing naturally; and

second, you are trying to make him *want* to do those things in the correct way.

It is of course impossible to force a horse to do anything. All you can do is to apply so much physical and moral pressure on him that eventually he will accede to your wishes. But first you have to make sure the horse is physically fit and well, since a half starved dejected animal is physically incapable of working freely and well. When you have him fit, he should naturally want to go forward, his head will come up, and he will be ready to start his schooling at the basic pace, the walk. The fitter he is the higher he will carry his head. If on the other hand he is being overfed, with too much corn, he will tend to refuse to walk at all; he will be dancing along, trying to get rid of the surplus energy that he has stored up. So by adjusting his feeding you can increase or decrease his energy. If he is slopping along with his head and tail down, it means that there isn't enough steam in the boiler, so the boiler needs stoking with more corn.

When you have got him walking at the pace you want, you can start thinking about improving his head carriage. Now the height of the head can be quite simply controlled by the height that you hold the reins. If you raise your hands, the horse's head will come up; if you lower your hands, his head will come down. If the horse's head is being carried too low, you have to raise his head slightly higher than you will want it eventually, because when his head is up, you can easily bring it down and in – always remembering that the horse's mouth is a very, very delicate thing and any pressure on it should be very gentle. If when you are riding you imagine you have an egg in your hand, and remember that if you squeeze too hard you will break the shell, you will have about the right pressure on the horse's mouth. When the neck is arched and the head has come down into the desired position, you will find that his quarters have also come under him. With good feeding you have increased his natural desire to go forward, so his hind quarters have gone forward, then by getting his head into the right position you have brought the head and the tail nearer to each other, so the horse will be carrying himself well. You will not of course be at his head and mouth all the time. To start with you will be quite happy if you can get him going correctly for fifteen or twenty yards. Then you let him relax again for half an hour. Afterwards you school him for another fifteen or twenty yards. By degrees, as his muscles develop, you will be able to extend the distance that he can happily and naturally carry himself.

Schooling is absolutely essential because it improves your riding. It is no good saying 'Oh! I don't need a schooled horse, I only want to hack round a bit.' It is always more enjoyable to ride a well schooled horse, even if you are just going down once a day for the paper. But it is essential to remember that the age of miracles is dead, and you must always be quite satisfied if he is going a bit better this week than last week.

Once you have improved the walk, you will find that the improvement follows quite easily into the trot, and the canter. And at the same time that you are improving the walk, you can also be changing any other annoying habits, such as not standing still when you get on, or taking a mile and a half before you can get him to halt.

Standing still for you to get on is a very easy habit to instil in a horse. You simply make him want to stand still. Again there are two or three ways you can make him do this. One of them is to put a bucket with a few nuts in it in the corner, and let him eat the nuts as you get on. Or you can get someone to hold him still in a corner when you mount. This is one of the things that you cannot deal with by having a battle with the horse, because if you do have a battle he will be dancing around so much that it will be *impossible* for you to make him stand still.

One of the tricks I use myself is to get a restive horse to stand with his head over a gate. Then I open the gate from his back and away I go. The advantage of this system is that the horse very quickly gets used to standing still in the gateway, and later he will stand still out of habit even when the gate is open, and eventually even when there is no gate there at all.

Teaching a horse to stop you use very much the same method. If you have a horse that refuses to stop when you tell him, it is quite simple to pull him round to that he is facing a fence or a solid object, so that he has to stop. This of course is a manoeuvre that you do at a walk: it is no damned good careering into a fence at a good long gallop and hoping he is going to stop for you to get off. He is just as likely to jump it, as I know from personal experience.

One of the tricks I used to employ in my youth to ensure that I was allowed to go where I wanted when out hunting, was to specialize in opening the gate for the Huntsman. This meant going flat-out up to the gate, skidding to a halt, jumping off and opening the gate for the Huntsman to go through. The Huntsman was thus quite pleased to see me going in front of him. I had a horse that was extremely good at this. I would gallop her flat-out at the gate, she would skid to a halt, I'd swing off and have the gate open and be away long before the Huntsman got to the gateway. This worked very well except on one day when my father had bought a new horse, and I took her out hunting the next day. At the first gate, as I tried to do my trick and started to swing off, Evette took off to jump the gate, and I went flying, ending up with my head between the bars of the gate, looking round like a prisoner in the stocks.

Having got your basic habits and the basic paces going well, you can proceed to get your horse jumping, and jumping well. The basic rules for teaching a horse to jump are these:

first, either the fence must be facing towards home, or several other horses must have jumped it in front of you;

second, the fence must look solid, and not over two foot high;

third, it must be made more or less impossible for the horse to run round it – which means it should be very wide, or in a gateway;

fourth, the horse must not be allowed to refuse.

As with schooling your horse walking, you will get the best results going towards home, simply because the horse knows that when it has done whatever you have asked of him he is going home to his dinner; or in company with other horses – by having a horse jump towards a group of horses, or following a group of horses over jumps. Both techniques give the horse an added wish to do what you want him to.

In all his early training, the horse must never be allowed to refuse. If he stops at a fence, he must not be allowed to turn his head from the fence. You can if necessary back two or three strides, for most horses can jump three-foot quite simply in three strides, and in the early stages you are not going to try more than eighteen inches to two feet, so that if necessary he can step over it. Once you allow a horse to turn his head away from a fence, you are encouraging him to refuse. When he is jumping two or three fences eighteen inches high one after another happily and well, you can start putting them up a couple of inches every three or four days. But make quite certain that if he makes a mistake, or is starting to get worried by the increase in height, you immediately drop the fence three or four inches and start again.

The whole time you are training your horse you should be increasing his desire to please you by giving him titbits and making a fuss of him every time he does something right. By this I don't mean he should be constantly rewarded when he is walking – you would expect him to do that perfectly before you praise him. But when he shows a certain amount of improvement, and you tell him what a clever fellow he is, you are developing his need for praise, and his need to excel, in order to earn that praise. And since you should be developing what he does all the time, a very great improvement can be seen quite quickly: a matter of weeks rather than months.

When you are jumping and cantering with other horses you should also be developing his desire to compete. For example when you jump him alone you should try to persuade him to do better each time; and when you jump him with other horses, you should be comparing his performance yourself with the other horses, competing against them all the time. In this way you will not only be developing the competitive side of his character, but your own competitive urge as well. And it is important to go into competition as often as you can, because this is the only way to measure how your training programme is proceeding. At the same time open competition will give an impetus and add a zest to your training.

12: *Royalty – A Short Case History*

We have now covered, through this book, the general principles of understanding what makes a horse tick, what makes him want to do some things and not others, and how these needs and desires can be used in the training of a particular horse so that he comes to want to do the things his rider wants. In this last chapter I am going to describe in detail my experience through one summer with Royalty, as the best demonstration I can offer of how I work from day to day with horses, and how I try with an individual horse to enter into his thinking – his psychology – in order to gain his goodwill and cooperation.

Royalty, whom I have already mentioned, came to us in the middle of June 1975 as an unbreakable and unmanageable four-year-old. And in the three months from the middle of June to the end of September, she progressed from being completely unmanageable to being able to take part in a small one-day event down in Pembrokeshire. We achieved this by using a combination of communication and psychology, both disciplines being seen as equally important halves of a whole. It doesn't matter how good your psychology is if the horse does not understand what you want him to do, and you do not understand without any ambiguity the horse's wishes and desires and feelings!

Royalty arrived while I was away, and the first time I went into her loose box she cowered in the corner saying, 'Oh! My God! here comes another horrible human. What's he going to do to me?' And as I went towards her she prevented me with her backside and told me in no uncertain terms that if I came near her she would kick me from here to Kingdom come. From this it was no feat of intuition to deduce that she had an antipathy for the human race. So the first thing to do was to reverse this, to transform her dislike and fear of human beings into a desire for my company.

At this time she was very restless in her box, and we realized that she had a great store of nervous energy, a need for movement, and a dislike of being confined.

Over the next forty-eight hours we also discovered that she would only eat about eight pounds of corn a day, and very little hay. Since she was pig fat we knew that she wasn't naturally a shy feeder, so it was obvious that the move and being shut in a stable had upset her digestion.

All these problems had to be overcome before we could get on to more serious work.

The feeding wasn't any problem at all, since we were reasonably certain that this would be overcome as she became more settled. Her dislike of a confined space we tackled by trying to make sure she felt safe in her stable, and making absolutely certain that anything likely to upset her was done elsewhere. For example when we shod her a week or ten days after she arrived, we did it in another stable. When we saddled her, we took her out of her own loose box, and the same when we groomed her, the first two or three times, until she began to enjoy being groomed. By this means, within a matter of days, her loose box, instead of being something that confined her, became a safe place for her to retreat to, and the far corner of the loose box became her own particular territory which was not invaded by me when she was in it.

It was obviously important that she should come to me and not me to her. So I put her food in that first night, but didn't give her any water. The following morning, before I put her food in, I went in with a bucket of water and put it on the floor, about three or four feet inside the stable door. Then I just stood outside the stable door, which I shut. Since she was thirsty she immediately moved towards the bucket, but then, seeing me, she stopped. Because I had the door shut, and I stood absolutely still, after two or three minutes she walked over and started to drink. As soon as she started to drink, I opened the stable door.

She retreated three or four steps and watched me. Again I stood quite still in the open stable door. She came over to the bucket after a bit and took three or four mouthfuls of water. Then I eased myself forward one stride; then two strides. Each time I moved she stopped drinking and retreated, but she always came back to the bucket of water. When she had finished, I took the empty bucket out, and put a small feed just inside the door. Again I shut the door. She watched me for a few seconds, then came over and ate the feed. So I left her to enjoy her breakfast, and went about my work.

I did the same thing again at dinner time. But this time as soon as I opened the stable door, she went back to her corner, and refused to come near the bucket of water. So I took it out and put her feed in, shut the door, and she came over and ate. By the evening of course she was very thirsty again, so I put the bucket of water just inside and stood outside with the door shut. After a minute or two she came over to the stable door, I opened it and she retreated a few steps. Then she came back and finished her bucket of water with me standing by it. I gave her more water, and she drank about half of the second bucket. When she had finished drinking, I took the water out, put her feed in again, put some hay in the rack and left her for the night, very pleased with the progress I had made in twenty-four hours.

The following morning when I put the bucket inside the stable door, she walked straight over to drink before I could even shut the door. As soon as she had drunk I gave her some more water, half of which she drank. Then I took the bucket out and put her feed in, and since she was very hungry for her breakfast, and she hadn't been hurt, and I hadn't done anything to frighten her other than stand in the doorway, she came over and ate her breakfast from the bucket, with me standing by her head. And all the time she was eating or drinking I talked to her in a sing-song voice, helping her to relax.

The third morning, when I went out first thing, she had joined in the chorus of the other horses and they all shouted 'Where's my bloody breakfast' together. So, in order to make the most of the progress that I was making, I varied the pattern very slightly. When I fed and watered her, instead of standing in the doorway, I stood just inside the door so that when she was drinking and feeding I would be standing just behind her shoulder. By now she had realized that I wasn't going to hurt her, and without any qualms at all on the third morning she went straight over to the bucket. First she drank and then she ate, then she alternated two or three mouthfuls with a sip of water to help wash the feed down. I did the same thing at lunch time, and when she was eating, I just let my fingers touch her body behind the shoulder. As soon as I touched her she jumped as if she had been branded with a red hot iron, but she didn't move back from the bucket, and after a second or two she put her head back down and I caressed her with the tips of my fingers, on her barrel, and on her shoulder. By the time she had finished eating I had my hand on her neck, and half-way up her neck along the ridge of mane, and was scratching her there in an itchy spot.

A couple of days more and I could go into her and handle her as and when I wanted, and I thought that I could start grooming her. So I led her out of her box into another, though still leaving her loose.

With a nervous horse like this, the first time I groomed her I would not use a brush. I used the method used by the Indian *sais*: he grooms a horse entirely by using his hands and his forearms, rather like a Swedish masseur. I always like to groom a young horse for the first two or three times in this way, though of course I don't put as much power and vigour into the movement as the *sais*, partly because I am too damned lazy, and partly because if I really pummelled the horse I should frighten the living daylights out of him. But on the other hand most horses quite like the rhythmic movement of my hands and arms going all over his body, and once they are liking this it is only a very slight change to having a body brush in my hands when I am doing it, and then to progress to using the body brush and brushing in the normal way, and finally to using a dandy.

By the end of a week Royalty's food consumption had gone back to normal, her restlessness had decreased considerably, and, provided no sudden movements were made, her nervousness had almost disappeared. Since she now liked and trusted me, I could go very quickly on to the next and more important stage.

So one day after lunch I moved her into the adjoining loose box and put a saddle and bridle on her. I did this without any difficulty, except that she arched her back when we tightened the girth, which about fifty percent of horses do when saddled for the first time. Then with the reins behind the stirrup leathers, and the stirrups flapping, we put her back into her own stall for the rest of the afternoon.

When we had had tea, we got out Rostellan and Irish Clancy – these are both big cobs with very fat, broad backsides – and Paddy and Mark, who were staying with us, got on the two cobs while I led Royalty into a very tight corner of the yard, which is where we like to mount horses the first time. She was actually in a passage six feet wide, with her head facing one building, another building on one side and railings on the other. In such a space a horse has no choice but to stand still when you are getting on to him, so someone held Royalty's head, and my wife gave me a leg up, easing me quietly up so that I was leaning across the saddle. Whilst I was doing so, I was talking to Royalty, and as soon as I got my arms over the other side of her I caressed her neck and flank with my hands. Her immediate reaction was something like 'My God, what the hell is he doing now.' But when she realized that I wasn't going to murder her, her natural trust of me reasserted itself and she relaxed. So I eased a leg over to the other side, sat up and put my feet in the stirrup. 'My God, what's happening,' she said, but I just talked to her and caressed her. My wife turned her round so that she was facing the other way, but still with the barrier of Rostellan's and Clancy's backsides blocking her path. We stood for a second, and I said 'Okay.' Paddy and Mark started their horses forward and Royalty followed them, half a length behind.

Paddy and Mark went out of the front gate and up the road towards the field where we have the horses running during the summer months.

All the time I was sitting relaxed, talking to Royalty and scratching her mane with my finger nail, which she liked. A couple of hundred yards up the road I said 'Stop.' Rostellan and Clancy halted, I said 'Whoa Royalty,' and gently squeezed the reins. Since there was no way past the two mountainous backsides in front of her, she had to stop. I said, 'Okay' again, the other two horses started forward, so I clicked my tongue and said 'Go on girl.' And of course she followed Rostellan and Clancy, going extremely sedately. A hundred yards or so more and I said 'Whoa' and touched the reins. The other two stopped and Royalty stopped. And we progressed in this manner the mile or so up to the field. By the last three or four times I said 'Whoa,' Royalty was stopping as soon as I touched the reins, before Paddy and Mark had stopped the other two horses.

A hundred yards from the field we stopped once more. Paddy jumped off Rostellan, gave her reins to Mark and came round and led Royalty the last hundred yards into the gateway, so that her head was over the gate. As soon as she was standing still, I gently slipped my feet out of the stirrups, and slipped to the ground. I unsaddled Royalty and held her while Paddy and Mark unsaddled their two horses and turned them into the field, and then I turned Royalty in after them.

The next couple of mornings Royalty came in quite happily with the other horses. And in the afternoon, after tea, before turning the others out, I rode Royalty to the field behind Clancy and Rostellan. On the second day for the last half-mile we alternated stopping and starting with walking and trotting. By the third day Royalty knew so well what was happening, that she gave a little bit of a wriggle and squeal as I turned round to go out to the field, and she did everything perfectly, stopping and starting when she was asked, and walking and trotting when told to do so. In fact about a quarter of a mile before we got there, she managed to get past the gigantic bottoms of Rostellan and Clancy and trotted down to the field by herself, stopping once without any difficulty. And when she got to the gate of the field, she jogged up to the gateway, stopped with her head over, and waited for me to get off and turn her out.

So within a single week we had changed a frightened, untouchable and unmanageable horse into one that was actually enjoying walking and trotting with someone on her back. And we had been able to do so because the task to be performed had been presented throughout in a natural progression and as a normal piece of equine experience. When we got on her for the first time, for example, and rode her, she could see the other horses being ridden and enjoying it, so she immediately realized that being ridden was a pleasurable activity, and not something to be frightened of.

The following morning – that is when we had had Royalty no more than a week – I decided to take her out when we were working the other horses. Quite by chance the direction we took went past the jumping lane, and since everyone else wanted to go up the jumping lane I asked them to come back to me on Royalty as soon as they had finished. But Royalty had other ideas. As soon as she saw the other horses disappearing up the jumping lane, she indicated that she wanted to follow and as I didn't want a battle, I decided I might as well let her. She belted into the first fence on Rostellan's tail, since he was at the back of the line. Rostellan popped over the fence, which was made of loose brush and about two foot high, and as he jumped Royalty was suddenly presented with what no doubt appeared to her to be a gigantic obstacle. Anyway, she put in a jump to match, shooting me several feet in the air – she went straight up and down again almost in the same place, and the heavy thump of me landing on her back was too much for her, so she put in two gigantic bucks, and this brought her to the next fence. Then, without thinking, she put in a third buck, which took her over the second fence, but this time I was ready for it. I didn't come down with a thump on her back, so she cantered quite nicely into the third fence, passing Rostellan on the way, and jumping the fence as to the manner born.

Since everybody, both human and equine, had thoroughly enjoyed the jumping lane, by unanimous decision we decided to go up it again. This time I decided to let her follow Biddy, since they were much of a size and pace, and Biddy went away with her customary dash and enthusiasm. Royalty followed, putting her best foot forward. She jumped the first fence perfectly, misjudged the second, sending loose brush flying all over the place, and went over the third with immaculate timing.

I decided that Royalty had done enough jumping for her fourth day mounted, so we continued our ride for an hour and a half, getting home in good time for dinner, elated that simply by allowing Royalty to use her natural talents we had got her jumping so happily within so short a time.

The following day the blacksmith was due to come, and since Royalty was getting a bit footsore, we decided we would have to shoe her. Shoeing a horse for the first time is always extremely important. If he gets hurt or frightened, or a battle is allowed to develop, bad habits can arise which persist for the rest of his life. So the following morning I took out a set of partly worn shoes that were just about Royalty's size. When Bryn came he took one look at her foot, altered the shape of the shoes slightly, and when he tried them they fitted her perfectly. Then without any fuss or bother he very quickly tacked them on, only putting five nails into each shoe. When he had nailed the four shoes on roughly, I held up one front foot whilst he clinched the other three shoes with Royalty's feet on the ground, the whole operation taking less than twenty minutes.

Whilst the shoes were reasonably firmly on, this technique did of course mean that she would have to be shod again in a couple of weeks. But when we shod her a fortnight later, we shod her hot, and since she had already been shod she knew what it was all about and there was no bother at all.

Over that fortnight, Royalty's education proceeded slowly but surely. I started doing a little bit of schooling on her, which meant that she was going out with the other horses for about two hours a day. As I rode I collected her by squeezing the reins so that her head had to come in. Since she wanted to keep up with the other horses, she collected her hind quarters under her. I did this every ten minutes or a quarter of an hour for a space of fifteen or twenty yards. At the end of about ten days the fifteen or twenty yards had been extended to forty or fifty, and by the end of about a month she was holding her head high and her body composed for a couple of hundred yards during every ride without any difficulty. Once she was walking collectedly for short periods, I got her trotting correctly too, which was very simple, and then cantering in the same collected way. Each time we used the impetus of her desire to stay with the other horses. I didn't need to use my heels or any other form of compulsion because the natural inclination was there, provided by the other horses. And all the time she was doing this she was also jumping fifteen or twenty small fences a day. By degrees the fences got bigger, and the type of obstacle changed slowly from a low brush fence to an even lower rail, then when she was jumping two or three low rails in succession we started raising them slightly.

At this stage Royalty was never asked to jump a fence by herself. She was always allowed to follow the other horses over it. But after about six weeks we began jumping her by herself. She had been jumping about three foot, but when we asked her to jump by herself we dropped the fences back to eighteen inches or two feet, and to make doubly certain we always jumped her towards a group of other horses. This we accomplished by letting the other horses jump the fences first, and then getting her to jump towards them a couple of minutes later. The next step was to get her jumping the line of fences away from the other horses, and when she had done this the other horses followed her. After that we had her jumping a dozen or fifteen fences in a circle, so that she went round in a circle away from the other horses, and then jumped back towards them. While she was doing this we very quickly got the fences back to about three foot, then increased them more slowly, until some of the fences were one-day event standard.

We had brought her to this standard rather more quickly than we would have normally. This was partly because we found we were merely developing her own very considerable natural desire to jump, and partly because we wanted to get her up to standard for a small cross-country competition we always ran at the end of August. The last fortnight or so my daughter Paddy took her over completely, riding and schooling her herself. And she rode her in the cross-country competition, doing extremely well with only a couple of stops at one of the bigger fences. Whilst this put her out for the prize money, we were delighted with her overall performance since she had done quite a good dressage test and a very good cross-country round.

Three weeks later Paddy took Royalty down to a one-day event in Pembrokeshire, finishing fifth out of twelve against some quite good horses. She did an extremely good dressage, had one stop at cross-country and one stop showjumping. This was absolutely fantastic when you remember that the first coloured fence she had ever seen she saw when she entered the arena to do her showjumping round. Paddy had asked my opinion of her prospects beforehand, and I had told her 'You will get round the cross-country, and do a passable dressage, but you are bound to get eliminated showjumping since Royalty has never seen a coloured jump in her life.' So for a very green four-year-old that was an excellent performance and we were extremely pleased with her.

The impetus her training had already given her had been reinforced by the two small competitions, neither of which had been of a particularly high standard but they had meant that the mare had to be ready to do a certain thing by a certain date. The standard she had reached was a little above average for the time, but it is this standard that is needed as a basis for any work. In the three months she had become an extremely good ride, going nicely and collectedly. And she could jump three-foot-six of solid timber, and small showjumps. Any horse following this routine and getting to this standard can go from there in any direction necessary. In Royalty's case I hunted hounds off her up until Christmas, and the sound groundwork of her basic training made her a superb hunter. She can now go one-day eventing in the summer, again building on the groundwork of her basic training. If she had been a thoroughbred she would have gone point-to-pointing in the spring, and because she had been properly schooled in the early stages she would have taken to it like a duck to water. And if I had been inclined to go show-jumping again the basic groundwork she had had would have been exactly right for showjumping. Biddy, who had gone through exactly the same regime of training, one-day evented last spring and last autumn extremely successfully.

The successful training of Royalty is typical of the use of good basic communication, and making the most of the horse's natural ability and desires (which is what equine psychology is about) to make training easy and satisfying for both horse and rider. And it shows, further, how a horse can be induced to achieve quite exceptional levels in competition in a remarkably short time. I hope that this book will have shown that by learning to 'think with' the horse, it is within the reach of any sympathetic horse-man or woman to gain new enjoyment and exceptional standards of performance.